DATE			
MAY 22 '86			

THE ECONOMY OF
Colonial America

THE ECONOMY OF

Colonial America

EDWIN J. PERKINS

COLUMBIA UNIVERSITY PRESS
New York   1980

LIBRARY OF CONGRESS CATALOGING IN PUBLICATION DATA

Perkins, Edwin J
The economy of colonial America.

Includes bibliographies and index.
1. United States—Economic conditions—To 1865.
I. Title.
HC104.P47   330.973′02   80-16478
ISBN 0-231-04958-7
ISBN 0-231-04959-5 (pbk.)

Columbia University Press
New York   Guildford, Surrey

Copyright © 1980 Columbia University Press
Printed in the United States of America

FOR MY FATHER
Paul

CONTENTS

PREFACE

MY interest in colonial economic history was stimulated several years ago when I was asked to review Joseph Ernst's *Money and Politics in America, 1755–1775*. The excitement of learning about eighteenth-century finance generated further curiosity about the status of scholarly research on other colonial topics. At the same time, I was dissatisfied with the books available to undergraduates on this era for my economic history course. Since no other historian had then published a summation and interpretation of recent scholarship in the field, I finally decided to embark on the project myself. Having written earlier a narrow monograph on the financing of nineteenth-century Anglo-American trade, and having subsequently compiled an edited anthology, I was predisposed to try my hand at a historical synthesis of some important period. Only later did I learn that Jim Shepherd and Gary Walton were already at work on a book focusing on the economic rise of colonial North America, with an emphasis on commerce. By then, I was already committed to the task.

The colonial era is appealing because it represents a study in contrasts. The economy was exceptionally dynamic in terms of population growth and geographical expansion. No major famines, epidemics, or extended wars intervened to reverse, or even slow down appreciably, the tide of vigorous economic expansion. From 1700 to 1774, for example, aggregate output multiplied almost twelvefold. At the start of the eighteenth century, the size of the colonial economy was a mere 4 percent of the mother country's; yet on the eve of independence the percentage had risen to over one-third, and the colonies were gaining steadily.

Despite this broad expansion, however, the fundamental patterns of economic behavior remained fairly constant. The members of the main occupational groups—farmers, planters, merchants, artisans, indentured servants, and slaves—performed similar functions throughout the period. In comparison with the vast number of institutional innovations in the nineteenth and twentieth centuries, structural change in the colonial economy evolved gradually. With the exception of the adoption of the pernicious system of black slavery, few new economic institutions and no revolutionary new technologies emerged to disrupt the stability of this remarkably affluent commercial-agricultural society. Although fluctuations in the size of harvests and in the level of foreign demand for colonial exports influenced the economy in the short run, the patterns of daily activities which developed in the seventeenth century generally prevailed until the 1770s. Living standards rose slowly but fairly steadily at a rate of 3 to 5 percent a decade after 1650.

This book contains a number of noteworthy features. Monetary sums are converted into 1980 dollars so that the figures will be relevant to modern readers. For example, the average per capita income level of £13 for the white population in the 1770s translates into $845 in 1980 prices. (See Appendix.) The focus is also primarily rural, reflecting the overwhelmingly agricultural nature of the economy. The family farmer thus receives the most extensive coverage in the section on occupational groups. In this context, I have stressed the similarities between the activities of farmers in the northern, middle, and southern colonies rather than their differences.

The most influential groups were the great planters in the south and the wealthy urban merchants in the north. Individual merchants and planters exercised more political power than economic influence, however. Compared to the twentieth century where big business, big labor, and big government all wield enormous economic power, the colonial world was governed far more by the free market forces associated with Adam Smith's classical economic principles. Governmental expenditures and taxes accounted for a negligible percentage of total gross production; labor unions were nonexistent; and business units were universally small. No individual or group of individuals possessed sufficient economic power to influence prices or restrict supplies of goods. In colonial society, impersonal market forces remained predominant.

For the most part, the book describes the economic life styles of free white society. The term "colonists" is virtually synonomous here with inhabitants of European origin. Thus, statements about very high living standards and the benefits of land ownership pertain only to whites. Occasionally I have added a qualifying statement at the end of a sentence such as "with the exception of blacks and Native Americans," but it could be validly inserted into almost every paragraph in the text. One chapter does focus exclusively, however, on indentured servants and slaves.

In addition, I often employ a comparative format, with conditions in the thirteen mainland colonies placed in a global framework or contrasted with trends in the modern world. Among the topics are demography, living standards, growth rates, wealth distribution, debtor-creditor conflicts, and the role of merchants and artisans in society. Unless otherwise stated, my vantage point in time is backward from the twentieth century, which is important in understanding why I lean so often on terms like "static" and "stable" in describing the economic life styles of the colonists. For the modern reader, who is caught up in a period of constant economic change, such a vantage point is, I believe, most effective in communicating how the earlier era differed from our own.

Several scholars went over various chapters and alerted me to additional sources, neglected facts, and questionable analysis. My close friend Frank Mitchell at the University of Southern California gave me excellent guidance early in the project. Oliver Rink added encouragement. Alice Hanson Jones kindly loaned me relevant prepublication chapters from her new book entitled *Wealth of a Nation To Be*, which Columbia University Press is publishing in 1980. Joseph Ernst, Paul Paskoff, Dennis Flynn, and David Galenson offered helpful critiques. My crosstown colleague at UCLA, Gary Nash, who views events in colonial America from a much different perspective, willingly shared ideas and data. Stanley Engerman volunteered to review the manuscript, and in a masterful and unbelievably helpful critique, he gave me innumerable suggestions for improvement.

xii PREFACE

This book represents my best judgment about the most important features of the colonial economy and their relationship to the general society and to the movement for independence. Hopefully, it will be a good starting point for all—undergraduate to scholar—interested in learning more about the seventeenth and eighteenth centuries. My bias has been in favor of the newer studies completed within the last two decades. My greatest debt is therefore to all the economists and historians who have been active in scholarship over the past quarter century. To me, they have been a source of inspiration, and I trust this volume will reveal the extent of their accomplishments to a much wider audience. While I tried to include a range of opinions on issues perennially debated, such as whether the independence movement had primarily economic origins or what roles various occupational groups like merchants, artisans, and common laborers played in the events of the 1760s and 1770s, in the end the emphasis and interpretation are my own.

Bob Rydell provided valuable aid in proofreading and the staff at Columbia University Press did an excellent job of managing all the editorial and production tasks associated with the book. Finally, I thank my wife Jan Bavouset for all her assistance and support.

THE ECONOMY OF
Colonial America

CHAPTER I

POPULATION AND ECONOMIC EXPANSION

THE colonial economy expanded at a dynamic pace throughout the seventeenth and eighteenth centuries primarily because of the spectacular growth of the free white and black slave populations. During the first century of settlement, the new arrivals were mainly Europeans from England and Holland. White settlers are estimated at 49,000 in 1650; by 1700 their number had grown to 223,000. Natural increase combined with continued immigration by Englishmen, plus the Scotch-Irish and Germans, brought the white population up to 1.69 million in 1770. After slavery had taken a firm hold in the southern tobacco colonies in the late seventeenth century, the size of the black population rose from around 5,000 in 1690 to 460,000 in 1770. Meanwhile, the native Indian population, which may have been as high as 300,000 in the eastern part of the continent at the start of the seventeenth century, declined precipitously. Some Indians were killed in hostilities, but most natives either moved further inland or died after contact with communicable diseases such as measles and smallpox, against which they had developed no natural immunities.

Each geographical region had a different pattern of population growth. New England received an influx of approximately 20,000 English settlers between 1620 and 1645; thereafter immigration virtually halted and natural increase was responsible for almost all of the region's subsequent expansion. The middle colonies attracted few settlers until late in the seventeenth century, and immigration played an important role in their development well into the eighteenth century. In the Chesapeake tobacco region, immigration from England was the source of growth through the 1660s. The white population was finally able to reproduce itself in the 1670s; and by the turn of the century, natural increase was the key factor in white population growth. For the black population, on the other hand, forced immigration continued at a rapid pace from 1680 through the 1740s. With the creation of a more settled slave society by mid-century, natural increase played the more vital role. After 1750, the impact of immigration—white and black—was greatly diminished, and natural increase was responsible for over 95 percent of the population growth in the thirteen mainland colonies.

On the eve of the Revolution in 1776, the thirteen colonies had a population of approximately 2.57 million, consisting of 1.95 million whites, 520,000 blacks, and 100,000 or fewer Native Americans. Virginia was the largest colony with 21 percent of the total population, followed by Massachusetts and Pennsylvania with 11 percent each. Philadelphia, with a population of from 30,000 to 35,000 citizens, was on a par with the five largest urban areas in England after London. On the basis of population, local political institutions, and underlying economic strength, the colonies were by no means dependent on Great Britain for survival by the mid-eighteenth century, and thereafter they increasingly resented English attempts, both in theory and practice, to view them in an inferior light. By the 1770s, the thirteen colonies already had one-third as many inhabitants as the mother country, and their overall economic output was almost 40 percent of Great Britain's. (See figure 1.1.)

The implications of American population and economic growth were not lost on Benjamin Franklin, one of the few colonials whose views on scientific matters and political affairs had a genuine following within the European intelligentsia. Franklin was an amateur demographer as well, and his commonsense predictions about the future course of American population and the reasons for its unusual growth have retained their relevancy. In his pamphlet *Observations Concerning the Increase of Mankind,* penned in 1751, Franklin pointed out that at the existing rate of natural increase, augmented by steady immigration, the colonies were doubling in size every twenty years. He added that colonial Englishmen and their slaves were destined to out-

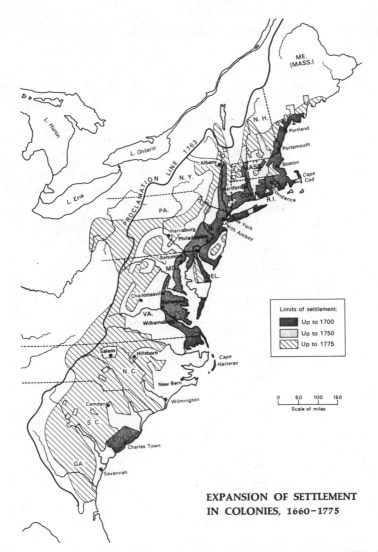

Limits of settlement:

- Up to 1700
- Up to 1750
- Up to 1775

0   50   100   150
Scale of miles

**EXPANSION OF SETTLEMENT
IN COLONIES, 1660–1775**

REPRINTED BY PERMISSION OF THE PUBLISHER, FROM JAMES A.
HENRETTA, THE EVOLUTION OF AMERICAN SOCIETY, 1700–1815 (LEX-
INGTON, MASS.: HEATH, 1973).

number the inhabitants of the mother country in a few more generations. Therefore, he foresaw pressure building to shift the balance of political and economic power within the British empire across the Atlantic to the colonies.

Franklin cited early marriage and larger families as the chief reasons for American growth. The typical number of children in a colonial family he estimated at around eight compared to only four in England and in the rest of Europe. Marriage was more frequent in the colonies too, he argued, because higher wages and the abundance of cheap land made it easier for a man to maintain a wife and raise a family. As indirect evidence of the greater economic opportunities in America, Franklin noted the absence of a permanent class of household servants; in England, persons in service were often forced by circumstance to delay marriage or to remain single.

Despite several instances of overstatement, modern studies of colonial demography have generally verified the fundamental soundness of Franklin's judgment. In accordance with the experience of most preindustrial societies, and many poor nations today, birthrates were very high. Only a small percentage of the population failed to marry. The colonial rate was between 40 and 50 births per thousand inhabitants, with some regions close to the historically biological maximum of 55 per 1,000 for a large population. Birthrates in Europe at the time ranged from 30 to 40 per 1,000. In a study of a wide sample of New England towns in the period from 1720 to 1760, Robert Higgs and Louis Stettler found that the number of children fathered by a married man was about seven on average, although it sometimes took a second or possibly even a third wife to reach that figure. One wife in six or seven died before the end of her fertile years, with childbirth and its complications probably the leading cause of death. (Husbands in their twenties and thirties apparently died at about the same rate from various causes.) The childless marriage was uncommon, and fewer than 15 percent of New England families had less than three children.

The age of the partners at marriage was lower in the colonies than in Europe. Americans typically married in their early and mid-twenties whereas contemporary Europeans often delayed marriage until their late twenties. Higgs and Stettler discovered that the average age of a woman at first marriage was 21, while for males the average age was 24. Teenage marriages and pregnancies were rare; it was unusual for a female to wed before 17 and a male before 20. Although the data are still fragmentary, there is nonetheless some evidence to suggest that the age of puberty for females was as high as 15 or 16 prior to the mid-nineteenth century, compared to 13 for American girls today. The late onset of fertility may well have accounted for the very low incidence of marriage for females in their mid-teens.

Just as Franklin had suspected, modern research on colonial demography has revealed a close correlation between early marriage and large families. Colonial households generally contained at least one more child than English households. In premodern Europe, and especially in Ireland, late marriage was the most effective means of limiting population, and even in the present era of sophisticated birth-control technology, the mainland Chinese have relied on delayed marriage as a major tool in slowing population growth.

Because of the high economic value of offspring in a society where labor was in strong demand, there is little evidence that colonial couples regularly practiced any method of birth control during the wife's most fertile years. In Europe, and especially in France, historians believe that coitus interruptus was commonly practiced in an effort to restrict the frequency of pregnancy. Even without safeguards, the normal interval between births was at least two years. The spacing was not a result of conscious attempts at family planning, but occurred because babies were invariably breast-fed and most women experienced lessened fertility during lactation. Some colonial women did, of course, give birth to fifteen or even twenty children, yet these cases were the exception not the rule. In Hingham, Massachusetts, from 1720 to 1780, Daniel Smith found that women who married before the age of 25 and survived multiple childbirth typically had three or four children in their twenties and four more after the age of 30.

While birthrates remained high for the white population, death rates were, in contrast, unusually low in comparison to the experience of other societies. Elsewhere in the world, high mortality rates offset the equally high birthrates and held down the growth of population. Whereas up to 40 persons per 1,000 died in Europe each year, in the thirteen colonies only 15 to 25 per 1,000 succumbed in the eighteenth century. Death rates fell sharply in New England in the seventeenth century and came down gradually in the southern colonies after the turn of the century. The exact reasons for the decline in death rates in the North American environment are still somewhat of a mystery.

Most scholars have cited three factors which, in combination, probably accounted in large part for fewer deaths. First, the colonists enjoyed abundant harvests, and the quantity and diversity in their diets made the settlers generally healthier and therefore more capable of warding off potentially deadly diseases. Secondly, a low population density discouraged the spread of communicable diseases; the incidences of exposure to smallpox, diphtheria, influenza, and other killers were reduced. No catastrophic epidemics were ever endured by the white and black populations on the mainland. Finally, plentiful supplies of wood fuel in most areas meant homes were warmer in winter—certainly warmer than in England where deforestation was extensive by the eighteenth century. Historians are in general agreement that advances in medical science and treatment were not among those factors contributing to the improved health of the population, since colonial doctors were in short supply and their training was often rudimentary. The absence of extensive health services was clearly no handicap given the limited medical knowledge of the period; in Europe, even the best-trained doctors could do little to prevent a high number of deaths from infectious diseases.

Perhaps the most important category where colonial demography differed from the European experience was in its lower infant mortality rate. The English death rate for children under the age of one was certainly no lower than 20 percent, whereas historians have discovered numerous regions in New England where only 10 to 15 infants in 100 failed to survive the first year. Again, scholars have attributed lower infant mortality rates to the good general health status of colonial women during pregnancy and throughout the nursing period. Fewer deaths among the young meant that a higher proportion of the population reached reproductive age, and that fact alone explains in large part why the colonies grew so rapidly.

After surviving infancy and adolescence, an individual's life expectancy was unusually long compared to standards in most other parts of the world. Indeed, life expectancies for young adults in certain New England towns, quite surprisingly, seem to rival the statistics on the current generation of Americans. In many regions, the average age at death for adult males was their early sixties. The data on adult females is conflicting. Some studies suggest a much lower life expectancy, with the explanation that deaths related to childbirth reduced the average age at death to the mid-forties. But Philip Greven in his widely respected study of Andover, Massachusetts, discovered that, over a span of four generations, adult women on average lived into their sixties as well. Moreover, Greven found that despite the assumed greater vulnerability of women during their childbearing years, in actuality more males than females died in their twenties and thirties in the Andover sample.

The demographic experience of blacks, both slave and free, was roughly the same as that for the white majority. By the 1740s, birthrates were likewise near the estimated biological maximum, and death rates were not much, if at all, higher than for whites. Aided by continued heavy importations of slaves in the eighteenth century, the share of blacks in the overall population rose from 8 percent in 1690 to 21 percent in 1770. The growth of black population on the mainland stands in sharp contrast to trends in the Caribbean and in the rest of Latin America during the colonial period.

In other parts of the western hemisphere where sugar or precious metals were the major product, the black population failed to expand through natural increase, and constant, forced immigration from Africa was required to maintain existing numbers. Birthrates were low and mortality rates were appallingly high—not only for slaves but for whites as well. Although questions remain about all the factors accounting for this demographic pattern, scholars have cited the following as characteristic of Latin American slavery: (1) the sex ratio was unbalanced with males outnumbering females, often by margins of 2 or 3 to 1; (2) the tropical climate played host to more diseases and the crowded conditions on many of the sugar islands provided a less healthful environment; and (3) the physical labor associated with sugar cultivation and mining was strenuous and sapped the strength of the average worker after a few years.

By the mid-eighteenth century, conditions in the thirteen mainland colonies were much different. The sex ratio was more evenly balanced, and a close approximation of the extended family model was the basis for social organization in slave quarters on the larger plantations. Allan Kulikoff found that *native born* black women typically married before the age of 20 and produced seven to eight children. Most blacks lived on relatively isolated southern farms, and like whites, their vulnerability to communicable diseases was low. Finally, the cultivation of tobacco and most food crops (except rice), while demanding and time consuming, was not physically debilitating for adults of either sex. Despite persistent myths, there is little evidence that slaveholders took arbitrary or abnormal steps to raise the rate of black fertility. Slaveholders presumably realized that artificial attempts to engage in "slave breeding" were superfluous, since by the 1740s the black population was already increasing at a very rapid pace.

Another long-overlooked factor which may have accounted for the sharp difference in fertility rates on the mainland and in the Caribbean has been recently singled out by Stanley Engerman and Herbert Klein. They found that female slaves in the West Indies normally followed the African custom of breast-feeding children for up to two years, whereas slaves on the mainland adopted the European practice of weaning babies within the first year. Since incidences of pregnancy are substantially reduced during the lactation period, this factor alone could account for a wide differential in child spacing. Moreover, some

African tribes had strong taboos against renewed sexual intercourse with a woman still breast-feeding her recent child. Engerman and Klein have suggested that these two factors may also explain in part why fertility rates for slaves were almost two times higher on the mainland than in the West Indies.

Given the size of the continent and the westward march of the frontier after 1776, the physical displacement of the native Indian population during the colonial years was remarkably slight. As late as the 1770s, European settlement was confined largely to a one-hundred-mile band stretching along the Atlantic Coast from Massachusetts to Georgia. Farmers tended to cluster within the main river valleys, so that even within the band of settlement, pockets of virgin forest remained where some Indians continued to live in mostly traditional ways. In the absence of any contrary evidence, we can assume that, in line with the pattern of most other pre-industrial societies, Indian birthrates and death rates were both quite high.

In New England, the native American population has been estimated at not much above 25,000 at the beginning of the seventeenth century, and most other regions were sparsely populated as well. Probably no more than 300,000 Indians lived within 150 miles of the Atlantic coast when the first European settlements were established, and the majority lived in the southern region. How many Indian tribes in contiguous areas were decimated after contracting communicable diseases like smallpox and measles is unknown, but most authorities have suggested that this inadvertent form of biological warfare was more responsible for native depopulation than any other single cause in the colonial period.

In the meantime, the black and white population, on the basis of an unusually high birthrate in combination with an unusually low mortality rate and steady immigration, grew at phenomenal speed, doubling every quarter of a century. The colonial demographic experience is roughly analogous to the situation existing in most underdeveloped countries in the twentieth century. In the poor nations of the world, birthrates of 35 to 50 per thousand, along with dramatically lowered mortality rates following the introduction of modern medical technology, have produced an explosion in world population. Like the age structure in the less-developed nations today, the colonial population was on average quite young, with one half under 18 years of age. By comparison, birthrates in the United States have fallen in the 1980s to close to the replacement level of 12 per 1,000; at present the median age is around 30, and it is destined to rise even higher in the decades ahead.

In light of the slow improvement in business technology and agricultural productivity in the seventeenth and eighteenth centuries, it is virtually impossible to overemphasize the importance of population growth in explaining the expansion of the colonial economy. Land and natural resources were abundant and already in place waiting for development. Labor was the scarce resource in the colonial era, and increases in the size of the labor force led to more extensive settlement and a corresponding expansion in the size and strength of the economy. Population growth was responsible for over 75 percent of the increase in aggregate economic output during the eighteenth century; the contribution from gains in per capita productivity was relatively low even on the basis of the most generous assumptions about their impact.

For every addition to the labor force, gainful employment was normally readily available. By modern standards the range of occupations was narrow, and most youths followed in the footsteps of their parents. Out of every 100 men who were employed, 80 to 85 became farmers, while the rest became skilled or semiskilled craftsmen, day laborers, or seamen; one individual might reach the status of merchant or great planter. In the urban areas, the wages earned by skilled workers and laborers were often 30 percent higher than, or even double, the rates paid for comparable work in England.

Transatlantic visitors constantly remarked about the few signs of poverty in the colonies. In England, a traveler invariably came across many beggers and paupers on rural roads and in the urban streets. Although scholars such as Gary Nash, Raymond Mohl, Allan Kulikoff, and James Henretta have discovered new data to show that public expenditures for poor relief in Boston, New York, and Philadelphia were increasing over the eighteenth century, nonetheless by European standards the colonies contained remarkably few persons who were abjectly destitute. Workers rarely remained unemployed for long periods of time, except the physically or mentally handicapped.

Despite the rapid rise in population, the typical colonial household was able to maintain its already very high material standard of living and even to make some improvements. The ability to hold up average living standards in the face of a population boom was a notable achievement. It was a genuine accomplishment that the thirteen colonies shared with England and Holland, and one that had rarely, if ever, been achieved by other societies prior to the seventeenth century.

Before 1600, economic expansion and population growth everywhere had invariably led to a decline in the amount of goods and services available to the average citizen. In Europe, where a large portion of the most fertile land was already under cultivation, increases in population were met by planting new fields that were marginally less productive. As a result, the average yield per acre fell, and the amount of food available for each member of the society was less. Eventually, a series of lean crop years produced widespread starvation; or, alternatively, a deadly disease, such as the plague, struck hard at an undernourished population and took away up to one-quarter, or in some cases one-half, of the inhabitants. Parodoxically, those who survived enjoyed improved living standards, since, with population reduced, only the more arable land was regularly cultivated. Soon a new Malthusian cycle of rising population, falling average incomes, and ultimate catastrophe began again.

But in the American colonies that cycle was avoided. As the colonial population rose, settlers were generally able to expand output on new lands that were no less fertile than existing fields. On the frontier, farmers cleared new fields that were more productive than the poorly maintained cropland they had abandoned near the coast. Even though population multiplied tenfold in the eighteenth century, food production per capita was clearly sustained. Indeed, food surpluses were so great in the late colonial period that overseas exports of grain, flour, and rice were on a rough par with the great southern staple—tobacco.

In the more settled areas along the coast, where population pressure caused a decline in the average farm size, most families pursued nonagricultural activities on a part-time basis and some even turned to a service or craft occupation permanently. Living standards were maintained since abundant and relatively inexpensive food could be imported from other regions with steady surpluses. There were no major crop failures nor devastating epidemics, nothing to diminish the optimism of the white settlers about the fundamental stability of their economic world. The colonists anticipated a continuous period of wellbeing, and the existence of seemingly unlimited new land to the west encouraged them to raise large families, since the opportunities for their heirs did not appear to be restricted by the natural environment.

In comparison with its more regulated European counterparts, colonial North America was a much closer approximation of the open, free-market society advocated by Adam Smith. In 1776, he published the classic *Wealth of Nations*, which soon became the oracle of capitalism because of its reliance on the unregulated price system to allocate economic resources. By eliminating artificial monopolies and other forms of governmental interference in the economy, and by generally allowing citizens to pursue independently their own self-interest, Smith argued that a given economy was more likely to approach its maximum potential for the production of goods and services.

Despite the inconveniences of some British economic regulations, which were often ignored and in any event affected no more than 5 to 8 percent of gross colonial output, the thirteen colonies largely fit the Smithian model. Given the existing technology and the availability of natural resources, this commercial-agricultural society was probably functioning at near maximum efficiency. Indeed, by the mid-eighteenth century, if not earlier, the typical white inhabitant of the mainland colonies was almost certainly enjoying the highest standard of living in the contemporary world.

BIBLIOGRAPHICAL ESSAY

There have been no similarly comprehensive studies of the colonial economy. Gary Walton and James Shepherd focus primarily on commerce and its contribution to economic expansion in *The Economic Rise of Early America* (Cambridge: Cambridge University Press, 1979). An earlier analysis of the underlying forces at work in the growth of the economy is Stuart Bruchey, *The Roots of American Economic Growth, 1607–1861* (New York: Harper & Row, 1968), although the primary emphasis is on the first half of the nineteenth century rather than the two earlier centuries. An excellent interdisciplinary overview of eighteenth-century history with a strong emphasis on ecomonic factors is James Henretta, *The Evolution of American Society, 1700–1815* (Lexington, Mass.: Heath, 1973). A paper that summarizes some of the recent literature is David Galenson and Russell Menard, "Economics and Early American History," *Newberry Papers*, No. 77-4E (Chicago: Newberry Library, 1978). For additional sources on income growth and economic development, see the references cited for the final chapter of this book.

A broad introduction to colonial population is found in Gary Nash, *Red, White, and Black: The Peoples of Early America* (Englewood Cliffs, N.J.: Prentice-Hall, 1974). Wilbur Jacobs surveys the debate about the size of the native American population in "The Tip of an Iceberg: Pre-Columbian Indian Demography and Some Implications for Revisionism," *William and Mary Quarterly* (January 1974), pp. 123–34. The black population of the western hemisphere is covered in Philip Curtin, *The Atlantic Slave Trade: A Census* (Madison: University of Wisconsin Press, 1969). An article that stimulated much of the recent interest in demography was J. Potter's "The Growth of Population in America, 1700–1860" in D. V. Glass and D. E. C.

Eversley, eds., *Population in History: Essays in Historical Demography* (London: Edward Arnold, 1965), pp. 631–88.

Two contemporary discussions of colonial population were Benjamin Franklin's 1751 essay, "Observations Concerning the Increase of Mankind," available in Leonard Labaree, ed., *The Papers of Benjamin Franklin* (New Haven: Yale University Press, 1961), 4:225–34, and Edward Wigglesworth's treatise, *Calculations on American Population, with a Table for Estimating the Annual Increase of Inhabitants in the British Colonies . . .* (Boston, 1775). Wigglesworth estimated that more Englishmen would reside in the new world than England by 1825.

Two recent books with extensive data on colonial population are Robert V. Wells, *The Population of the British Colonies in America before 1776: A Survey of Census Data* (Princeton, N.J.: Princeton University Press, 1975); and Alice Hanson Jones, *American Colonial Wealth*, 3 vols. (New York: Arno Press, 1977).

Much of the scholarly work on colonial demography has focused on New England. The most comprehensive studies of the region are Daniel Scott Smith, "The Demographic History of Colonial New England," *Journal of Economic History* (March 1972), pp. 165–83, and Robert Higgs and Louis Stettler, "Colonial New England Demography: A Sampling Approach," *William and Mary Quarterly* (April 1970), pp. 282–94. Maris Vinovskis concentrates on a single colony in "Mortality Rates and Trends in Massachusetts before 1860," *Journal of Economic History* (March 1972), pp. 184–213.

Many recent studies analyze small towns or counties: John Demos *A Little Commonwealth: Family Life in Plymouth Colony* (New York: Oxford University Press, 1970); Demos, "Families in Colonial Bristol, Rhode Island: An Exercise in Historical Demography," *William and Mary Quarterly* (January 1968), pp. 40–57; Demos, "Notes on Life in Plymouth Colony," *ibid.* (April 1965), pp. 264–86; Philip Greven, *Four Generations: Population, Land, and Family in Colonial Andover, Massachusetts* (Ithaca, N.Y.: Cornell University Press, 1970); Greven, "Family Structure in Seventeenth-Century Andover, Massachusetts," *William and Mary Quarterly* (April 1966), pp. 234–56; and Kenneth Lockridge, *A New England Town, The First Hundred Years: Dedham, Massachusetts* (New York: Norton, 1970).

Wesley Frank Craven covers one southern colony in *White, Red, and Black: The Seventeenth-Century Virginian* (Charlottesville: University Press of Virginia, 1971). Allan Kulikoff focuses on the black population in the tobacco regions in "A 'Prolifick' People: Black Population Growth in the Chesapeake Colonies, 1700–1790," *Southern Studies* (Winter 1977), pp. 391–428, and "The Origins of Afro-American Society in Tidewater Maryland and Virginia, 1700 to 1790," *William and Mary Quarterly* (April 1978), pp. 226–59, while Terry Anderson and Robert Paul Thomas discuss mainly white indentured servants in "The Growth of Population and Labor Force in the 17th-Century Cheaspeake," *Explorations in Economic History* (July 1978), pp. 290–312. A comparative study is Herbert Klein and Stanley Engerman, "Fertility Differentials between Slaves in the United States and the British West Indies," *William and Mary Quarterly* (April 1978), pp. 357–74. See also Engerman and Robert Fogel, "Recent Findings in the Study of Slave Demography and Family Structure," *Sociology and Social Research* (April 1979), pp. 566–89.

For comparative data on Europe, see Carlo Cipolla, *Before the Industrial Revolution: European Society and Economy, 1000–1700* (New York: Norton, 1976); E. A. Wrigley, *Population and History* (New York: McGraw-Hill, 1969); and Daniel Scott Smith, "A Homeostatic Demographic Regime: Patterns in West European Family Reconstitution Studies," in Ronald Lee, ed., *Population Patterns in the Past* (New York: Academic Press, 1977), pp. 19–51. One recent article on England is David Loschky and Donald Frier, "Income and Family Size in Three Eighteenth-Century Lancashire Parishes: A Reconstitution Study," *Journal of Economic History* (September 1969), pp. 429–48.

For an excellent assessment of the status of research on colonial demography plus a comprehensive list of sources, see Daniel Scott Smith, "The Estimates of Early American Historical Demographers: Two Steps Forward, One Step Back, What Steps in the Future," *Historical Methods* (Winter 1979), pp. 24–38. An outline of a major research project covering a broader time period is Robert Fogel et al., "The Economics of Mortality in North America, 1650–1910: A Description of a Research Project," *ibid.* (Spring 1978), pp. 75–111.

CHAPTER II

FOREIGN TRADE

L IKE other European nations with overseas empires, the British expected their colonies to serve the mother country and to pursue economic activities that on balance contributed to the power of England vis-à-vis its continental rivals. The reigning economic orthodoxy of the day was mercantilism, a rather fluid term (like modern Keynesianism), which advocated self-reliance and a favorable balance of international trade. With the sale of goods overseas exceeding the aggregate purchases of foreign products, other nations would be forced to settle their deficit accounts through the shipment of specie—gold or silver. According to mercantilist precepts, specie inflows per se strengthened the political and economic power of the recipient and simultaneously weakened those countries losing gold and silver. It is noteworthy that twentieth-century economists generally favor the maintenance of a favorable trade balance as well, although the goal is no longer to attract gold, since its possession is now considered of little special value, but rather to boost employment levels in the home country.

In the mercantilist world view, colonies were expected to assist the mother country in promoting a favorable balance of trade. The British colonies in the new world might help in several ways. First, a colony could contribute directly to England's strength by purchasing semifinished and manufactured goods over and above the value of the raw materials and foodstuffs it shipped to the home market, with the deficit balance paid in specie. Colonies could also contribute by growing a product such as tobacco which the mother country could sell in large quantities to the inhabitants of continental powers, thereby draining rivals of their specie. Finally, the colonies could contribute by supplying products within the empire, such as sugar and lumber, which England otherwise would have purchased from external sources.

To guarantee that trade flows were in harmony with the perceived requirements of the empire, the colonial powers normally adopted regulations designed to steer commerce into the proper channels. For the first half of the seventeenth century, when the population of Europeans on the mainland was less than 50,000, Parliament had permitted its colonies to engage in unrestricted trade with the French, Spanish, and the Dutch, who had a small colony of their own in New York until 1664. Beginning in the 1650s, however, Parliament passed a series of Navigation Acts, which established the ground rules for colonial participation in world trade. The major provisions of the acts were as follows: (1) they excluded vessels registered in foreign countries from the carrying trade between ports strictly within the British empire; (2) they provided that manufactured goods from continental Europe could not be imported directly by the colonies but had to pass through England first; (3) they authorized bounties for colonial products especially desired in the home market; and, finally, (4) they specified that certain products deemed extraordinarily valuable in international trade were "enumerated," which meant that shipment only to England or other British ports was permitted. Among the items placed on the list of enumerated goods were furs, ship masts, rice, and tobacco.

One of the longest-running debates between economic historians revolves around how seriously these various Navigation Acts damaged the colonial economy and whether resentment over their enforcement was a prime cause of the rift with England in the 1760s and 1770s. The consensus now is that the net burden on the colonies did not exceed 1 to 2 percent of total income in any given year. The trade regulations tended to benefit northern shipping interests, who were protected from competition with French, Spanish, and Dutch vessels. The producers of indigo in the lower south received bounties for growing plants which yielded dyes valued in the British textile industry. On the other hand, tobacco growers in Virginia, Maryland, and North Carolina were penalized because they were prevented from selling their product directly to buyers on the continent, where prices were invariably higher than in England. The extent of the planters' losses was far less than the price differential between Britain and the continent, however, since the English and Scottish tobacco merchants provided valuable merchandising services. Indeed, in the years after independence and the ending of trade regulations, most U.S. planters continued to market their tobacco though the British mercantile network voluntarily. The maintenance of old marketing patterns after political separation suggests that the *real* impact of trade regulations on tobacco growers was not very great.

Meanwhile, all regions enjoyed the protection of the British navy on the high seas, and Parliament often reimbursed the colonies for expenses incurred in the course of conducting military operations against various Indian tribes and the French. On the whole, protests about British restrictions on overseas trade played a negligible role in stirring up revolutionary sentiments. The colonists' protests were directed rather at the sharply increased taxes which were a new feature of Parliament's commercial acts after the conclusion of the French and Indian War in 1763.

The northern colonies lacked the resources to yield valuable products unique to the western hemisphere; thus they failed to conform quite as well to the imperial model as their southern counterparts. Since the northern climate was fairly similar to England, mercantilist policymakers viewed these colonies skeptically. They were potential competitors of the mother country as well as possible benefactors. The agriculture was much the same, with basic foodstuffs predominating.

The basis for direct trade with England in the seventeenth century was restricted largely to furs, fish, and ship masts. Furs became an export from New England soon after the Pilgrims landed at Plymouth in 1620. The Pilgrims used their earnings from the fur trade to pay the debts incurred in sailing to the new world and provisioning themselves during the first few years. In the 1630s, the Puritans, who had established a much larger settlement in the Boston area, took over the fur trade, and they dominated it until beaver were virtually hunted to extinction in New England before the end of the seventeenth century. The decimation of the beaver population in the northeast was one obvious manifestation of how the economic activities of Europeans had a strong negative impact on the natural environment.

In the eighteenth century, the center of the fur trade shifted to New York. The Hudson River and its tributaries made connections with regions that were still largely wilderness as late as the 1770s. To prevent their shipment by Dutch descendants to merchants in Holland, furs were put on the enumerated list in 1722. The fur trade represents one field of endeavor where economic cooperation between the native Indian population and Europeans was sustained over a long period of time. By the mid-eighteenth century, however, furs were an insignificant item in the export totals.

When the English arrived in New England, virgin forests covered up to 90 percent of the land, and some settlers may have envisioned the development of an extensive timber trade with the mother country. By the seventeenth century, England had undergone an extended period of deforestation, and wood, which was the primary source of construction material for homes, buildings, and ships plus a major source of energy for household heating and iron manufacturing, was already in short supply. England was heavily dependent on suppliers in northern Europe and Scandinavia for timber products, and political leaders considered this reliance a handicap for a strong naval power. But transportation costs were too high to justify the opening of a general transatlantic trade in lumber with the colonies.

Tall and straight white pines, sometimes reaching a height of 120 feet, were prized as ship masts, however. English shipwrights could use a single tree to fashion a mast for a large ship that was much stronger than those pieced together from shorter European trees. White pines meeting the proper specifications eventually became enumerated products, and government contracts for supplying the royal navy with ship masts were one of the rewards savored by successful political factions in Massachusetts and New Hampshire. The enforcement of British rules limiting the cutting of trees designated by a carved arrow in the bark as solely the property of the Crown proved extremely difficult in the deep forest, and conflicts between imperial officials and colonial poachers, who valued the pines for shingles, clapboard, and barrel staves, persisted into the eighteenth century. For military reasons, the royal navy valued the northern colonies as a secure source of masts in the event of war on the European continent, but in strictly economic terms, the mast trade with England generated only modest revenues.

By the late colonial period, northern exports to Great Britain were still severely limited. The two most important products were, oddly, whale oil and potash. The whaling industry expanded swiftly after 1750; twenty years later over 250 vessels set sail each season from northern ports in search of whales. Before the rise of the petroleum industry in the middle of the nineteenth century, whale oil was valued for illumination and lubrication; it was used to finish leather and to make soap, and the head matter of sperm whales produced the fine quality candles. Potash, or pearl ash, was another forest product. After burning three to five acres of timber, workmen could leach the ashes with water and extract a ton of potash, a chemical used in the manufacture of soap and glass.

The northern colonies were much more valuable to England as an overseas market for home manufactures. Textiles and metal hardware were the leading exports to the colonies, both north and south. The importance of the colonies in the export trade of the mother country escalated in the eighteenth century. In 1701 the American colonies (including the West Indies) took only 10 percent of England's domestic exports, but by 1772 the figure had risen to 37 percent. In 1772, for example, Great Britain exported goods valued at £1,720,000 ($112 million) to the northern colonies alone; British imports from the same region were only £115,000 ($7.5 million), leaving a favorable trade balance of £1,605,000 ($104 million) for the mother country. (For the monetary conversion methodology, see Appendix.)

The British concern about potential competition from colonial manufacturing was well founded, for northern businesses were able in a few fields to produce adequate supplies not only for colonial consumption but also to make inroads into the English home market as well. Thus, Parliament periodically enacted new legislation designed to limit the right of the colonists to engage in economic activities that threatened competition with a significant number of English craftsmen and manufacturers. The goal was to discourage American manufacturing and to preserve colonial markets for home industries, but that proved difficult to achieve. Parliament was able to prevent the colonies from exporting manufactured goods back to England and to other foreign ports; however, it generally failed to deter the colonists from producing finished goods for local markets.

The first colonial enterprises seriously affected by export restrictions were hat manufactures. Concentrated mostly in the Hudson River valley, colonial hatters produced beaver-fur hats that, by 1730, had captured a sizable share of the European market. In retaliation, British hatters persuaded Parliament to pass the Hat Act in 1732. It made illegal the exports of colonial hats on the grounds that the jobs and profits of Englishmen took precedence over any benefits accruing to colonial entrepreneurs and European consumers.

The British attitude toward the emerging colonial iron industry was, in contrast, more tolerant. The natural inclination to slow the acquisition of manufacturing capabilities in the colonies was partly offset by the desire to diminish the mother country's increasing dependence on Sweden for the iron ingots from which metal products were fabricated. The deforestation of England was an environmental factor which had restrained the production of iron, because wood charcoal was the only energy source technologically perfected for use in the refining process. (Coking coal was also technologically adapted late in the eighteenth century.)

The mainland colonies had virtually unlimited timber resources in the vicinity of ore sites, and beginning with the establishment of a furnace at Saugus, Massachusetts, in 1645, colonial iron production rose to 1,500 tons annually, or around 2 percent of world output by 1700. In the next century the center of production shifted to Pennsylvania, and by 1775 the colonies were a major producer of iron, accounting for about 15 percent of world output. The colonies exported to Great Britain pig and bar iron valued at roughly £50,000 ($3.25 million) per year in the pre-Revolutionary decade, with about equal amounts from the middle colonies and the upper south.

Because of shortages at home, the British encouraged the establishment of iron furnaces in the colonies, but Parliament still attempted to reserve for English workmen the privilege of fabricating the metal into useful products. The law passed in 1750 eliminated all customs and duties on bar and pig-iron shipments to England on the one hand, and it simultaneously forbade the construction of any new facilities in the colonies for fabricating iron into finished products. This ban on the establishment of new fabricating shops was blatantly ignored by the colonists and invariably with the implicit support of royal governors, who normally sought to avoid confrontations with local political leaders and merchants, and who had no means of effectively enforcing the prohibition in any event. By the 1770s, Pennsylvania, Maryland, and New Jersey had over a hundred locations where iron and some steel products were turned out for colonial consumers.

From the perspective of the twentieth century, one of the most serious deficiencies in the mercantilist outlook on economic affairs relates to the proper role of manufacturing in the colonial empire. The accepted view was that the growth of manufacturing in the colonies represented a threat to business interests in the mother country and therefore Parliament was obligated to discourage such activities. Among the eighteenth-century students of political economy who suspected this line of mercantilist reasoning needed closer examination was, again, Benjamin Franklin.

In a pamphlet written in 1760, he argued that the British fear about competition emerging within the empire was largely misplaced. The bulk of England's trade was actually with her continental rivals, Franklin observed, and these nations had already begun to develop the manufacturing sectors of their economies. The basis for commerce between prosperous nations with similar economic structures was

broader than between nations with wide disparities in environment, incomes, and productive capacities. "A man must know very little of the
trade of the world," Franklin wrote, "who does not know, that the
greater part of it is carried on between countries whose climate differs
very little." Therefore, he concluded, England probably had far more to
gain than to lose from the expansion of colonial manufacturing.

Once more Franklin's commonsense reasoning has proven compatible with modern theory and practice, for greater opportunities exist today for commerce within the circle of industrialized nations, where incomes are high, than between those wealthy nations and the
underdeveloped and poor countries, where purchasing power is low.
Because of the expansive nature of the colonial economy, aggregate
imports from England reached all time highs in the pre-Revolutionary
years.

With limited opportunities for exporting directly to England, the
northern colonies looked elsewhere for foreign markets. They discovered strong demand for their surplus products in the Caribbean
sugar islands and in southern Europe and the Wine Islands. The trade
regulations placed few restrictions on the shipment of fish, grain,
livestock, lumber, staves, and other basic provisions to ports outside of
England.

In the 1640s and 1650s, the New England colonies established trading patterns which prevailed throughout the colonial era. The
Puritans and their descendants supplied provisions to island societies
which concentrated almost exclusively on the cultivation of staples—
sugar in the Caribbean and wine grapes in the European outposts off
the coast of northwestern Africa. By the eighteenth century, the
middle colonies of Pennsylvania, New Jersey, and New York had
entered this trade as well, and shipments were now extended to Medi-
terranean ports, particularly along the southern coast of Spain.

By the 1770s, the trade routes were firmly established. The data in
table 2.1 reveal that the middle colonies shipped primarily bread,
flour, wheat, and salted beef and pork to southern Europe and the
West Indies. The New England colonies sent dried fish to

TABLE 2.1.   Balance of Trade with Selected Regions: Middle
Colonies, 1768–1772 (mean average in sterling)

Exports to	West Indies	Southern Europe	Great Britain
Bread & flour	£171,000 76%	£132,800 73%	—
Wheat	—	32,400 18	—
Beef & pork	14,200 6	—	—
Iron	—	—	£ 24,000 36%
Potash	—	—	12,200 18
Other	38,800 17	17,600 9	30,400 46
	£224,000	£182,800	£ 66,600
Imports from			
Rum	£102,400 46%	—	—
Sugar	61,000 28	—	—
Molasses	42,000 19	—	—
Wine	—	£ 22,500 69%	—
Salt	—	9,700 31	—
Other	15,600 7	—	£822,200 100%
	£221,000	£ 32,200	£822,200
Net exports or (imports)	£3,000	£150,600	£755,600

SOURCE: Tables 1–13 (pp. 211–36), in James Shepherd and Gary Walton, *Shipping, Maritime Trade, and the Economic Development of Colonial North America* (Cambridge: Cambridge University Press, 1972).

southern Europe while their exports to the Caribbean included fish, horses, pine boards, cattle, spermaceti candles, and a variety of other products (table 2.2). By the late colonial period, New England no longer exported flour and grain; Massachusetts actually imported wheat from the other colonies.

From the West Indies, the northern colonies imported mainly rum, molasses, and sugar. In the Caribbean commodity trade, the mainland colonies actually purchased more goods than they sold. Most of the rum was consumed in the colonies, since alcohol consumption per capita was very high. The remainder was shipped largely to New-

TABLE 2.2.   Balance of Trade with Selected Regions: New England,
               1768–1772 (mean average in sterling)

Exports to	West Indies		Southern Europe		Great Britain	
Fish	£ 94,700	34%	£57,200	87%	£	—
Horses	53,900	19	—		—	
Pine boards	39,700	14	—		—	
Cattle	19,500	7	—		—	
Candles	18,200	6	—		—	
Beef & pork	15,600	6	—		—	
Whale oil	—		—		40,400	52%
Potash	—		—		22,400	29
Other	36,400	14	8,400	13	14,200	19
	£278,000		£65,600		£ 77,000	
Imports from						
Molasses	£141,300	48%	—		—	
Rum	74,800	25	—		—	
Sugar	40,400	14	—		—	
Salt	—		£11,000	61%	—	
Wine	—		7,000	39	—	
Other	38,300	13	—		£670,200	100%
	£294,400		£18,000		£670,200	
Net exports or (imports)	(£16,400)		£47,600		(£593,200)	

SOURCE: see table 2.1.

foundland, where rum consumption per capita was even higher. The
alleged rum-for-slaves trade with Africa was generally a myth. Little
rum left the thirteen colonies for Africa, and few colonial ships
regularly engaged in the transatlantic slave trade. Similarly, the so-
called triangular trade between the northern colonies, the West Indies,
and England was in truth quite small. The vast majority of vessels
sailing from colonial ports for the Caribbean returned directly home
without ever leaving the hemisphere.

The northern colonies generated large surpluses in the commodity
trade with southern Europe. The return cargoes of wine and salt were

valued at little more than one-sixth of the export figures for foodstuffs. The middle colonies had on average an annual favorable balance of trade of £150,600 ($9.8 million) from 1768 to 1772. As a result, the colonies built up substantial credit balances with mercantile firms in the Mediterranean, and those funds were subsequently transferred to London, where they helped to finance the heavy volume of colonial imports from England. Despite these earnings from the southern European trade, the northern colonies were in an overall deficit position in their international commodity accounts because of their unfavorable trade balances with the West Indies and, particularly, with Great Britain.

The New England and middle colonies paid for these excessive imports primarily with the funds earned in providing shipping and financial services for a large percentage of the North Atlantic overseas trade. Economists call these "invisible" earnings because they fail to appear in the statistical data compiled on imports and exports. Gary Walton and James Shepherd have shown that these invisible earnings were by no means inconsequential, however. Indeed the northern colonies earned on average more funds from the carrying and insuring of cargoes than from any tangible commodity. Colonial ships dominated the West Indian trade, and they played a major role in the commerce with England and southern Europe. In 1772, for example, invisible earnings amounted to £740,000 ($48 million) for the northern colonies and covered 50 percent of the deficit in the commodity trade.

The southern colonies fit more readily into the mercantilist mold. They not only provided a growing market for English manufactured goods, but they also produced specialized crops which were heavily in demand in England and on the European continent (table 2.3). The upper south, consisting of Virginia and Maryland, contributed tobacco; this luxury item was actually not used extensively by Englishmen but was sold instead to French, German, and other European consumers. Thus tobacco became a major factor in determining Britain's trade balance with its European rivals. In addition, planters in South Carolina had become large suppliers of two other crops

TABLE 2.3.   Balance of Trade with Selected Regions: Southern
Colonies, 1768–1772 (mean average in sterling)

Exports to	West Indies		Southern Europe		Great Britain	
Tobacco	—		—		£ 766,100	63%
Rice	£ 56,000	29%	£ 51,000	33%	198,600	16
Indigo	—		—		112,400	9
Wheat	—		58,500	38	—	
Bread & flour	31,800	16	27,000	18	—	
Indian corn	48,200	25	—		—	
Boards & staves	39,800	20	—		—	
Other	18,500	10	16,900	11	136,500	11
	£194,300		£153,400		£1,213,600	
Imports from						
Rum	£100,500	65%	—		—	
Sugar	27,100	18	—		—	
Molasses	15,500	10	—		—	
Wine			£ 16,700	99%	—	
Other	11,300	7	100	1	£1,336,300	100%
	£154,400		£ 16,800		£1,336,300	
Net exports or (imports)	£39,900		£136,600		(£122,700)	

SOURCE: see table 2.1.

highly valued in Europe—rice and indigo. Like tobacco, rice was extensively reexported to northern Europe, while indigo was prized at
home as a dye in the British textile industry.

The expansion of the economy in the upper south corresponded
with the rising demand for tobacco in England and on the continent.
The discovery that Virginia's sandy soils were especially well suited
for growing high-quality tobacco transformed the colony in the 1620s.
From a struggling settlement on the verge of starvation and abandonment, Virginia's economy boomed in the early 1620s when the price of
tobacco temporarily skyrocketed. Although prices declined sharply in
the 1630s, profits were substantial enough to attract a continual stream

of new free immigrants and white indentured servants into the Chesapeake area.

From 1640 to the end of the century, the tobacco trade expanded steadily. Black slaves began to replace white indentured servants in the labor force after the 1680s. Then, in the first quarter of the eighteenth century, production stabilized and the vigor of the Chesapeake economy was tempered. Jacob Price argues that this period of stagnation was not caused by limitations imposed by an inadequate supply of labor or by soil exhaustion in the older areas, but rather reflected a momentary lull in the growth of foreign demand for tobacco. After 1725, demand revived and grew at a steady pace until the 1770s, and Price links the renewed prosperity of the upper south economy with the spurt in demand generated primarily by the French market. In the late colonial period, the French government, which exercised monopoly rights in purchasing overseas supplies, bought heavily through Scotland's Glasgow tobacco merchants. After 1730, Glasgow merchants had diverted much of the tobacco business away from London, because their agents in Virginia and Maryland were prepared to offer spot cash at the wharf for a planter's crop, and because they granted liberal credit terms to their colonial customers. Between 1740 and 1770 the population of Virginia rose from 180,000 to 450,000, while tobacco exports jumped from £165,000 to £476,000 ($10.7 to $30.9 million).

In South Carolina and in the small Georgia settlement, rice and indigo were staple crops cultivated widely for the export trade. Over the last half century of the colonial period, the value of these two crops increased rapidly and by the early 1770s exports were £312,000 ($20.3 million) annually for rice and £117,000 ($7.6 million) for indigo, or combined slightly over 50 percent of the value of tobacco.

Because the English government appreciated the great value of colonial rice and tobacco in international trade, these two products headed the list of enumerated goods. All tobacco shipments went to Great Britain, where English and Scottish merchants reexported up to 85 percent of the crop to continental buyers. Similarly, all rice destined for ports in northern Europe also had to pass through

Britain. Roger Ransom has calculated that if the colonists had had the opportunity to send their crops directly to continental ports, bypassing Britain completely, then their proceeds from foreign trade would have increased substantially. In 1770, for example, he estimates southern revenues might have been as much as £446,000 ($29 million) above the £852,000 ($55.4 million) figure actually recorded, or 52 percent higher. In terms of the overall impact on the colonial economy, the enumeration of southern staples imposed by far the greatest burden. Indeed, the southern colonies assumed roughly 90 percent of the gross burden of around £565,000 ($36.7 million) associated with the Navigation Acts, and regional income may have been penalized as much as 2.5 percent annually.

Ironically, the financial burden connected with enumeration regulations dwarfed in size the new direct taxes Parliament imposed in the pre-Revolutionary decade. The English government had hoped to raise no more than £40,000 ($2.6 million) per year from taxes on official stamps, tea, and other colonial imports. Despite the heavy burden on the southern colonies, planters rarely complained about the navigation laws and rarely cited them as a grievance during public debates over the American role in the British empire. Moreover, despite the enumeration handicap, southern planters had higher incomes and held more wealth than northern farmers and many urban merchants. In South Carolina the percentage of slaves in the population was much higher than elsewhere, and the value of exports per white settler was the highest on the mainland by a wide margin. As a result, white South Carolinians enjoyed the best living standards in the thirteen colonies, and Charleston contained the largest collection of wealthy inhabitants, many of them absentee rice and indigo planters who preferred to spend one-half of the year in the city.

By the 1770s, the sale of food surpluses overseas was the most rapidly expanding export sector for the south. In respect to their attitude toward enlarging foreign markets for surplus food, the southern colonies had more goals in common with their northern counterparts in the late colonial period than before 1730, when tobacco was the unchallenged southern export. Rice had become a crop of major importance by the mid-century. In response to rising world prices for foodstuffs, wheat and corn production in Virginia and Maryland was boosted and sizable amounts became available for sale in foreign markets.

In Virginia, grain exports per capita rose by over 300 percent after 1740, whereas tobacco exports per capita moved up by only 17 percent. David Klingaman has shown that grain exports jumped from £11,500 ($750,000) in 1740 to £130,000 ($8.5 million) in 1770; and by the later date, the overseas shipments of foodstuffs were 25 percent of the sterling figure for tobacco. Much of the grain came from new lands which were better suited for food crops than for tobacco.

Settlers opened up the Shenandoah Valley in Virginia, just west of the low-lying Blue Ridge Mountains. The valley soils were ideal for wheat, and farmers had access to distant markets by shipping grain down the Shenandoah River, which flowed north to the Potomac. In Maryland, the counties contiguous with Pennsylvania were also more adaptable to grain cultivation, and the high quality of Maryland flour created a strong demand in the Caribbean sugar islands. The high world prices for food encouraged many planters in the settled tobacco regions to shift more land and manpower into wheat production for foreign markets.

Since the export of staple crops was so important to the economy of the lower colonies, historians have too frequently forgotten to emphasize that the production of foodstuffs for personal consumption was still the chief source of real income for southern as well as northern farmers. With few exceptions, rural families ate more of the food they produced than they sold on domestic and foreign markets.

Even prior to 1750, the south was self-sufficient in food. More acres were planted in food crops, especially corn, than in tobacco on even the most specialized Chesapeake plantations. Most families, free and slave, maintained vegetable gardens and some livestock. In this respect, mainland plantation slavery differed sharply from Caribbean sugar estates, where little food was grown and provisions had to be

constantly imported. Klingaman has estimated that the total value of
the corn and wheat grown in Virginia between 1768 and 1772 was
£864,000 ($56 million) annually compared to tobacco production of
only £493,000 ($32 million) annually. About 90 percent of the corn
crop and 83 percent of the wheat harvest was consumed within the
state, with the remainder exported mainly to the Caribbean. This
increased diversification of agriculture was a key factor in maintaining, and even augmenting, living standards in the upper south during
the eighteenth century.

As the population of the southern colonies rose from 115,000 in
1700 to 1.2 million by the 1770s, the region became an increasingly
important outlet for English manufacturers. The south imported goods
valued at £1.6 million ($104 million) from Great Britain in 1772, or
16 percent of the mother country's overseas commerce. The southern
colonies ran huge trade deficits with England, which coincided nicely
with mercantilist policy. However, they also generated substantial surpluses in the trade with Scotland because active Glasgow merchants
had captured a large share of the Chesapeake tobacco trade by the
early 1770s. As a result, the southern commodity trade with Great
Britain as a whole was near equilibrium, with the excess funds accumulating in Scotland mostly transferred to London to finance colonial imports of English goods.

Among the most misunderstood and misinterpreted economic
developments in the late colonial period relates to the possible role of
planter indebtedness to British mercantile firms in fomenting the
movement for political independence. Historians have often suggested
that resentment over large debts to foreign merchants and the hope of
eventually escaping the repayment of outstanding accounts probably
had a strong influence on the attitude of planters toward a possible
break with the mother country. A close examination of the functioning
of the merchandising and financial system for handling southern
staples indicates that these alleged economic motives for separation
have been grossly overrated.

The extension of credit to southern planters was a device employed
by British merchants, operating in a highly competitive market, to at-

tract business. British merchants earned commissions and profits first
on the sale of a planter's produce in the home market and then on the
return shipment of finished goods ordered by the planter. Indeed,
some scholars believe that the main source of profits for British
merchants serving the Chesapeake area came not from tobacco
transactions per se but rather from high markups on textiles,
hardware, and luxuries sent back to the colonies.

In the last two colonial decades, British merchants offered increasingly liberal credit terms to southern planters, large and small. In Virginia, for example, Emory Evans estimated that outstanding debts in
the neighborhood of £2 million ($130 million) were owed by up to
35,000 individuals, with most accounts below £100 ($6,500).
Increased debt was not a sign of economic weakness or accelerating dependence, but rather evidence that planter and merchant alike were
confident about the future prosperity of the southern colonies. The
southern grower normally went into debt voluntarily. An optimist, he
often used borrowed funds to buy more land and slaves.

Depictions of desperate planters burdened with uncontrollable debts
are misleading. The settlement of accounts was rarely that difficult.
Many of the goods ordered from England were not necessities but
belonged in the luxury class, and simply by curtailing for a year or so
the volume of overseas purchases, a grower's debts could usually be
painlessly discharged. In certain years, like 1772, monetary disturbances in Britain caused a brief period of credit stringency and led to
strained relations between growers and merchants, but these mild
crises failed to disrupt the basic trading and financial patterns. Of
course, some planters overextended themselves in acquiring land and
slaves on borrowed money and then had to liquidate those assets when
tobacco prices dropped or crops failed. Nonetheless, the image of the
southern planter saddled with mounting involuntary debts to English
merchants which could be paid only with great sacrifice should be ex-
cised from historical accounts of the late colonial period.

In general, the mainland colonies thrived within the British empire.
Most settlers were never too distant from water transport facilities, thus
they had ready access to regional and foreign markets. Indeed the

colonists were fortunate to possess two attributes which virtually assured success in an agricultural-commercial society: an endless supply of fertile land given the size of the population and a reasonably efficient distribution system to exchange their agricultural surpluses for tropical crops and goods manufactured at home and overseas.

Meanwhile the colonies were not seriously damaged when Parliament enacted a series of Navigation Acts. From one angle, the colonies did suffer losses, since, without any restrictions whatsoever on bilateral trade with other countries, the prices paid for European imports would have been lower and the prices received for some exports, especially tobacco out of the upper south, would probably have been higher. On the other hand there were substantial benefits associated with participation in the empire. The government offered bounties for certain products like indigo. The British navy provided protection at sea for all imperial vessels, and at no direct cost to the colonists. By the mid-eighteenth century the incidents of piracy had declined sharply, and the colonists were able to cease their reliance on armed merchantmen and to construct new vessels, without heavy guns, that were less expensive and had more cargo space. With risks curtailed, insurance rates declined. The drop in freight rates and other distribution costs aided the colonial economy.

Colonial shipowners were also permitted to participate fully in the empire's North Atlantic trade. Along with shipowners in the mother country, they enjoyed protection inside the empire from competition with the Dutch, French, Spanish, and other outsiders. The colonists quickly captured a large share of the lucrative North Atlantic trade. The major American ports were busy commercial centers. Boston and Philadelphia, for example, had perhaps 20 to 25 percent of their workers employed in commerce and fishing, with another 5 to 10 percent involved directly in shipbuilding. Ship construction was a flourishing colonial industry, with American shipwrights supplying not only the regional demand for vessels but also selling up to 45 percent, or £140,000 ($9.1 million), of their annual production to overseas buyers in the 1770s.

Yet no analysis of the costs and the benefits of colonial status versus a hypothetical free-trade model can highlight sufficiently the general benefits accruing from a close, and often intertwining, association with the economy of a mother country which was itself expanding at a very rapid rate for an early modern society. Population was rising in England too, and per capita incomes grew steadily in the eighteenth century, with only the yearly rate of growth—0.3 up to 1 percent—still in doubt. By comparison, France and Spain, two other European powers with extensive hemispheric interests, were not experiencing similar economic development. Britain and its mainland colonies were expansive economic societies, which stimulated and reinforced one another's progress. On both sides of the Atlantic, merchants and entrepreneurs were permitted greater social status than in most other contemporary societies. The English inheritance of political and economic institutions gave a fairly free reign to individual initiative and encouraged the colonists to seek property and wealth.

Despite the undeniable importance of the foreign-trade sector, we should nonetheless keep in mind that it only involved around 9 to 12 percent of colonial gross output. Overseas commerce based on the comparative advantages of regional specialization clearly raised income levels, but the real strength of the colonial economy was its prodigious agricultural production for local consumption and urban centers. The value of goods and services for strictly internal consumption outweighed by over 800 percent the volume of colonial exports. Even without the stimulus of foreign markets, living standards in the eighteenth century would have still ranked among the highest in the world, primarily because of the availability of so much fertile and productive land for the existing population—topics discussed in the following chapter.

At the same time, it would be a mistake to de-emphasize too much the role of the foreign-trade sector, especially if we take into account its influence on the institutional development of colonial society. Without overseas demand for tobacco, rice, and indigo, it seems questionable whether the institution of slavery would have spread from the Caribbean to the mainland. Slavery was linked to specific crops, not to a certain climate. Also important was the impact of foreign trade on one very critical part of colonial society—the economic, social, and political elite. The vast majority of individuals in the highest income category, primarily urban merchants and great planters, accumulated wealth as a result of their involvement in foreign commerce. Irrespective of how marginally foreign commerce affected the lives of the typical farmer, it had a substantial impact on the top 10 percent of wealthholders. Colonial political leaders were drawn in disproportionate numbers from the elite economic classes. Therefore the vagaries of overseas trade had a much broader influence on the political activities and concerns of the colonial legislatures than was probably justified on the basis of its effect on the income of the average citizen. Because of their close ties with the economic elite, issues related to foreign trade played a disproportionate role in the political affairs of the thirteen colonies.

BIBLIOGRAPHICAL ESSAY

James Shepherd and Gary Walton, *Shipping, Maritime Trade and the Economic Development of Colonial North America* (Cambridge: Cambridge University Press, 1972) is a gold mine of statistical data on foreign trade from 1768 to 1772. Indeed, it is probably the most valuable book now in print on the colonial economy, and I relied on it heavily in this chapter. Their select bibliography lists most of the important contributions on colonial commerce.

The literature on the net effect of the Navigation Acts is extensive. A sample of important contributions includes Oliver Dickerson, *The Navigation Acts and the American Revolution* (Philadelphia: University of Pennsylvania Press, 1951); Lawrence Harper, "The Effects of the Navigation Acts on the Thirteen Colonies," in Richard Morris, ed., *The Era of the American Revolution* (New York: Columbia University Press, 1939), pp. 3–39; Robert Paul Thomas,

"British Imperial Policy and the Economic Interpretation of the American Revolution," *Journal of Economic History* (September 1968), pp. 436–40; and Roger Ransom, "British Policy and Colonial Growth: Some Implications of the Burden from the Navigation Acts," *ibid.*, pp. 427–35. Benjamin Franklin's views on the inappropriateness of limiting colonial manufacturing are found his essay, "The Interest of Great Britain Considered," written in 1760 and published in Benjamin Labaree, ed., *The Papers of Benjamin Franklin* (New Haven: Yale University Press, 1961), 9:47–100. The quoted passage is on p. 77.

For information on New England trade and manufacture see Bernard Bailyn, *The New England Merchants in the Seventeenth Century* (Cambridge, Mass.: Harvard University Press, 1955); Douglas McManis, *Colonial New England: A Historical Geography* (New York: Oxford University Press, 1975); Thomas Norton, *The Fur Trade in Colonial New York, 1686–1776* (Madison: University of Wisconsin Press, 1974); Edouard Stackpole, *The Sea-Hunters: The New England Whalemen during Two Centuries, 1635–1835* (Philadelphia: Lippincott, 1953); and Charles Carroll, *The Timber Economy of Puritan New England* (Providence, R.I.: Brown University Press, 1973).

Important articles which focus on the Chesapeake region are Russell Menard, "Secular Trends in the Chesapeake Tobacco Industry," in Glenn Porter and William Mulligan, eds., *Economic Change in the Chesapeake Colonies* (Greenville, Del.: Eleutherian Mills, 1978); Edmund S. Morgan, "The First American Boom: Virginia 1618 to 1630," *William and Mary Quarterly* (April 1971), pp. 169–98; Jacob Price, "The Rise of Glasgow in the Chesapeake Tobacco Trade, 1707–1775," *ibid.* (April 1954), pp. 179–99; Price, "The Economic Growth of the Chesapeake and the European Market, 1697–1775," *Journal of Economic History* (December 1964), pp. 496–511; Emory Evans, "Planter Indebtedness and the Coming of the Revolution in Virginia, 1776 to 1796," *William and Mary Quarterly* (October 1962), pp. 511–33, and "Private Indebtedness and the Revolution in Virginia, 1766 to 1796," *ibid.* (October 1971), pp. 349–74; and David Klingaman, "The Significance of Grain in the Development of the Tobacco Colonies," *Journal of Economic History* (June 1969), pp. 268–78. See also Allan Kulikoff, "The Economic Growth of the Eighteenth-Century Chesapeake Colonies," *Journal of Economic History* (March 1979), pp. 275–88.

Other valuable studies with a broader focus are Jacob Price, "Economic Function and the Growth of American Port Towns in the Eighteenth Century," in Donald Fleming and Bernard Bailyn, eds., *Perspectives in American History* (Cambridge, Mass.: Harvard University Press, 1974), 8:123–88; Richard Sheridan, "The British Credit Crisis of 1772 and the American Colonies," *Journal of Economic History* (June 1960), pp. 161–86; and Geoffrey Gilbert, "The Role of Breadstuffs in American Trade, 1770–1790," *Explorations in Economic History* (1977), 14:378–87.

Section One

OCCUPATIONAL GROUPS

FROM a functional and institutional standpoint, the economic life of the thirteen colonies was remarkably stable. During the entire colonial period, occupational roles changed very slowly. The vast majority of the male population fit into one of six categories: family farmer, planter, indentured servant, slave, artisan, and merchant. A seventh category would include unskilled day laborers and seamen in the larger port cities, but scholarly research on these inarticulate groups remains fragmentary despite some progress in the last decade. Each occupational group performed economic functions in the 1770s in much the same manner as in the prior century. Occasionally, occupational roles overlapped; for example, farmers engaged in handicraft production in the off-season, and planters sometimes acted as merchants in their relationships with smaller neighbors. But from the perspective of the twentieth century, the range of occupations was narrow and rigid.

In the seventeenth century, when settlement had just begun, upward mobility was common in many regions. Indentured servants, bound to service for four to seven years, worked off their debts and moved on to new positions, sometimes acquiring substantial wealth. By the eighteenth century, however, social, economic, and occupational mobility had declined, and a more ordered, hierarchical society had emerged. Still, except for blacks and the few remaining Indians, individuals were faced with more opportunities for material and social advancement than in Europe.

CHAPTER III

FARMERS AND PLANTERS

THE basic economic unit in colonial America was the farm. Up to 85 percent of the population depended on agriculture for their livelihood. In following this pattern of rural employment, the colonies differed little from contemporary societies around the globe, for productive land was the most valuable economic resource in all pre-industrial societies. Yet special circumstances permitted the colonial farmer to achieve an unusually high standard of living. The size of the typical colonial farm was generous, often 100 acres, and families consistently grew and harvested surpluses. Equally important, farmers had access to adequate transportation facilities and thus had the opportunity to exchange their surplus production for handcrafted and manufactured goods in active markets both at home and abroad.

A majority of colonial farmers owned outright the land they tilled. Fertile land was not a scarce resource in North America, and it could be acquired at relatively low prices. Some colonists received title to land free of charge, for example through the headright system which granted every emigrant 50 acres in Virginia or through the division of formerly common property in a New England township. In unsettled frontier areas it normally took hard physical labor and some incidental funds to convert raw land into arable farms. In the eighteenth century, the value of improved land in older regions near markets rose substantially; in southeastern Pennsylvania prices jumped almost 300 percent between 1730 and 1760. On the frontier, new land was always plentiful, however, and irrespective of historical accounts about vast speculative ventures, land prices remained competitively low and well within the means of the average citizen.

Tenancy rates were as a rule much lower in the mainland colonies than in most other agricultural societies. In England, rural property was concentrated in the hands of the gentry who lived off the rental income. The freeholder class—owner-occupiers with title to 40 acres or more—held only about one quarter of English farmland. In most regions over 80 percent of all farm workers were tenants or itinerant laborers. Similarly high tenancy rates were common in most regions of Europe and Asia. As late as the mid-eighteenth century, many English tenants tilled plots in common fields rather than on farms with permanently fixed boundaries.

The English upper classes relied on this pattern of land tenure to restrict the franchise. Voting rights were extended only to freeholders. In the colonies, however, implementation of the same 40 acre rule left political power squarely in the hands of the average white, male farmer.

Only in New York were tenancy rates comparable to those in the Old World. The Dutch had created a series of vast estates in the Hudson River valley in the first half of the seventeenth century, and the British continued the estate system after gaining control of the colony in 1664. Despite institutional similarities, the relationship between landlord and tenant differed significantly in New York from European practice. Sung Bok Kim has shown that lease terms were normally quite reasonable, since reliable tenants were in short supply and landlords were interested in promoting settlement on their property. Many tenants were granted leases in perpetuity, with 10 percent of farm output commonly fixed as the annual rental. Even these modest rents were often difficult to collect. Leases were also transferable, and established tenants with improved lands were frequently in a position to sell their rights to new settlers at a solid profit. New York tenant farmers were hardly a downtrodden class; substantial numbers enjoyed a standard of living roughly on a par with freeholders in other colonies.

In a new study of Springfield, Massachusetts, from the 1650s to the turn of the century, Stephen Innes found that almost one-third of the town's adult males rented farmland. The vast majority of these renters already owned a farm of their own, however, and only leased to supplement their existing holdings. The average leasehold was around 15 acres, which was 20 to 40 percent of the size of the typical farm in that area. Only about 10 percent of the Springfield sample could be classified as genuine tenant farmers, with no other source of income.

Innes's data point up a frequently misunderstood fact which bears on the interpretation of colonial tenancy rates. Tenancy was by no means a condition linked solely with the desperate and poverty-stricken; it was, alternatively, a strategy for enterprising young men and new arrivals with little capital but a strong capacity for work to acquire sufficient funds over perhaps a three- to five-year period to purchase a farm of their own. Unlike Europe, where most of the population was locked permanently into tenancy, in the mainland colonies tenant status was often only a temporary stepping-stone toward the rank of property holder.

Nonetheless, scattered evidence indicates that the rate of tenancy was probably increasing in many areas during the late colonial period. In a recent study of Maryland, Gregory Stiverson concluded that a class of downtrodden tenant farmers, trapped in near subsistence agriculture, had already emerged. In some Maryland counties which had been settled for several generations, half of the farmers were landless tenants by the 1770s. They cultivated the poorest lands and typically had large households of eight or more members. Movement to the frontier, where land was usually very cheap, was a potential escape route, but most Maryland tenants were reluctant to migrate because of kinship ties at home and the continuing Indian threat.

Despite reports of tenancy rates of 30 to 50 percent in parts of Maryland, Pennsylvania, and New York, there is no solid evidence that the incidence of tenancy was approaching this magnitude throughout the colonies. In many areas of the south, tenant farmers sometimes owned one or two slaves and were clearly rising in the economic structure. For every family permanently stuck in tenancy, several others were merely passing through tenant status, on a full or very often partial basis, with the genuine prospect of subsequent economic independence. Tenancy in the colonial setting was as often a path of upward mobility as a condition of hopeless dependency.

In colonial North America the bulk of the land was owner-occupied, and consequently the distribution of wealth by European standards was surprisingly widespread, even in the south. Peter Lindert and Jeffrey Williamson have shown that the distribution of wealth in agricultural areas changed very little over the eighteenth century. By and large, productivity gains and increases in property values accrued to those families that actually worked the land, with the exception, of course, of black slaves.

Despite regional variations in soils and climate, farmers everywhere grew sufficient food to feed generously their immediate families and to provide an adequate diet for servants and slaves. The picture of southern farmers dependent on the production of an inedible staple for survival has been overdrawn; in Virginia, Maryland, and North Carolina more acreage by far was planted in corn and other grains than in tobacco. In the south and elsewhere, the largest and most valuable portion of a farmer's output was consumed right on the farm. Colonial farmers planted a mix of corn, wheat, barley, oats, and rye, plus numerous vegetables in season; they invariably raised livestock as well—cattle and hogs for meat, hides, and dairy products; horses for transportation; and sheep for wool. The degree of crop diversification seems to have increased in the eighteenth century, especially in the upper south. As a rule, only a part of a farmer's land holdings were under cultivation in a given year. On a typical family farm of 75 to 125 acres, perhaps 15 to 35 acres were actually planted in crops; the remainder was a combination of pasture and forest.

By European standards, the colonists appeared backward and unsophisticated in the application of farming techniques. Little attention was given to maintaining or enhancing the fertility of cultivated land. Fertilizers were applied sparingly, and fields were not plowed or were plowed superficially. The wooden plows were rarely plated with iron or steel coverings. Nonetheless, one agricultural historian, Conway Zirkle, has argued that in many areas in the New World deep plowing would have been inappropriate. After centuries of forestation the virgin soil was rich in humus, and extensive plowing actually would have caused a faster decline in fertility. The heavy concentration of tree roots in recently cleared land also made plowing exceedingly difficult. Since most colonial farms had large stretches of uncultivated land in forest or pasture, it was a rational economic decision to plant one field for a few seasons and, when its initial fertility began to subside, to move on to another plot.

After a long fallow period, the old fields normally regained their productivity. Indeed there was no steady decline in the fertility of most colonial farmland, including the tobacco-growing region of the upper south. Individual fields were temporarily exhausted, but the overall agricultural output of a typical farm of 75 to 125 acres was not seriously impaired. New England appears to have been the exception, for the soil was poor from the start and population pressure reduced the size of the average farm below the acreage required to sustain fertility without more systematic care.

An indigenous crop—maize or corn—was a mainstay in the colonial diet. Before the seventeenth century, many Indian tribes near the Atlantic coast had relied heavily on corn for survival. Early European settlers seeking arable land came across many open spaces that the Indians had previously cleared for cornfields. The native Americans introduced Europeans to a distinctive method of cultivation. Young corn plants were "hilled"—that is, soil was hoed up around the base. The Indians showed the colonists how to place dead fish inside the hill to serve as fertilizer. They sometimes practiced multiple cropping too. Bean seeds could be planted in the hills, with the cornstalks performing double duty as bean poles.

Corn was normally one of the first crops planted by new settlers. Based on the technique of hill cultivation, it was adaptable to fields not fully cleared but containing dying girdled trees and stumps. Corn was a hardy crop as well, for it was quite resistant to local diseases and insects. Farmers thus counted on it as reliable insurance against a serious setback in the event other grain crops fared poorly. For a small family with limited labor resources, corn was a sensible crop, because, unlike wheat, its harvest season extended over a fairly long period of time.

A highly adaptable plant, corn was cultivated extensively from New

England to Georgia. One worker was capable of tending 6 to 8 acres and producing 80 to 120 bushels, or enough corn to feed five to seven persons a year. On most farms, surplus corn was fed to livestock, especially hogs. The same procedure of fattening swine with corn is followed on today's farms as well.

Wheat was another important crop in the thirteen colonies. The various strains of spring and winter wheat, and other grains, were of European origin. In the middle colonies and some counties in the upper south, wheat was the main crop, since it served not only as the primary source of food on the farm but as the region's principal export as well. Consumers at home and abroad preferred baking with wheat flower over corn or rye flour, and they willingly paid higher prices for it. In Boston markets the price of wheat was typically 35 to 85 percent above corn in the eighteenth century, according to Karen Friedmann.

In the seventeenth century, spring wheat had been widely and successfully cultivated in New England. The appearance and spread of the wheat blast, now identified as black stem rust, reduced yields sharply, however, and led many farmers to shift to less tasty but hardier rye strains. Rye was nutritionally a good substitute for wheat on the farmer's table, but unfortunately a poor economic substitute because overseas demand was limited for rye.

While wheat fields were becoming less prevalent in New England, they expanded significantly in the tobacco-growing regions of the south. Chesapeake farmers discovered that winter wheat harmonized well with other plantation crops. In All Hallow's Parish, Maryland, Carville Earle found that winter wheat was planted in early fall after the tobacco had been harvested and before the gathering of late corn. The wheat required little attention over the winter and its harvest in June or July came after tobacco plants had been transplanted.

Wheat had a shorter harvest season than corn in all areas, because, once the grain began to ripen, the farm family had to cut it quickly or risk spoilage in the field. Labor resources were thus critical during the harvest season, and wages for temporary workers, if they could be found, were high. A farmer's wife and children normally put in a full day's work at harvest. Wheat yielded from 5 to 12 bushels per acre in settled counties up and down the Atlantic coast. As a rule, families had more land than they could farm, since they were able to plant and grow more grain than they were physically able to harvest. The introduction of the cradle scythe around 1750 boosted production capacity somewhat, but bottlenecks in harvesting technology prevented the emergence of specialized commercial wheat farms. The increased productivity in agriculture came in the nineteenth century after the development of major improvements in harvesting technology, such as the horse-drawn reaper.

In addition to wheat, corn, and rye, a colonial farmer was likely to plant a few acres of buckwheat for his family, some barley for brewing beer, and oats and hay for livestock. Diets were supplemented with garden vegetables in season, and some farmers maintained small orchards, especially apple trees in cooler climates. There were other regional variations, of course; the white potato did better in the north, while the more nutritious sweet potato fared better in the south.

The colonial farm normally had a varied livestock. The heavy consumption of milk, cheese, and meat was a key sign of the relative affluence of the colonial population. James Lemon has calculated that some farmers in southeastern Pennsylvania could afford the luxury of feeding up to 60 percent of total grain production to their livestock. Robert Mitchell estimated that the bulk of the corn grown in Virginia's Shenandoah Valley went to feed animals. The average adult farm resident ate from 150 to 200 pounds of meat a year, or about half a pound a day. By comparison over a billion people living in underdeveloped nations today rarely consume meat more often than once a week and many suffer from serious protein deficiencies.

Cattle and swine were the main sources of meat in colonial diets. These animals were European imports, for the Native Americans kept only domesticated hogs. Pork remained more important than beef because it was more safely preserved by salting and smoking. The typical farm in the middle colonies probably kept 6 to 10 hogs and 5 to 8 cattle. Swine were also easier to raise since they were capable of foraging for natural food on unimproved land and of protecting themselves from marauding wolves and other predators. Cattle needed better pasturage, and many varieties of English grasses and clovers were introduced in the seventeenth century to replace the less-satisfactory native grasses. In addition to meat, some cows provided milk, although daily production was low by modern standards; a cow that gave over one quart per day was considered a good milker.

Other livestock on the farm were oxen, horses, sheep, and chickens. Oxen were used in some areas as plow animals. Horses were kept for both plowing and transportation. Sheep were prized mainly for their wool rather than their meat. Wool could be transformed into clothes and blankets in the home and sold in the market. Chickens provided meat and eggs. Both poultry and sheep were highly vulnerable to natural predators, however, and had to be closely watched.

Besides growing sufficient food to provide an ample and reasonably nutritious diet for his family, most colonial farmers also produced for the market. The extent and nature of agricultural surpluses varied according to climate and soils. In the prosperous southeastern counties of Pennsylvania, James Lemon estimated that the typical farmer in the late colonial period had 40 percent of his total output available for sale. In the Shenandoah Valley, Robert Mitchell put the figure at 25 percent during the 1760s. David Klingaman's data suggest that 45 to 50 percent of total farm production of corn, wheat, and tobacco in Virginia was normally sold in overseas markets. Corn and wheat output totaled £864,000 ($56 million) annually in 1768–72, with about 15 percent, or £130,000 ($8.5 million) exported, while tobacco production was £493,000 ($32 million) with virtually the entire crop exported. In other regions where land was less productive, such as in New England or in areas distant from active commercial centers or good transportation, families were closer to subsistence farming and the volume of output entering the marketplace was much lower.

In addition to the sale of surplus crops, farmers often earned supplementary income from a variety of outside activities. In the middle colonies, farmers produced a substantial amount of flaxseed for the

Irish linen market, while South Carolina planters grew indigo for the English textile industry. The forest was another major source of extra income. In New England, some farmers turned hardwood ashes into potash, felled tall pines for the mast trade, or sold firewood in nearby towns and villages. Hundred of miles to the south, farmers in North Carolina relied on the production of naval stores—tar, pitch, and turpentine—for additional funds. A number of rural residents were part-time craftmen, and many fabricated barrels and other wood products in the winter months.

In the northern colonies and parts of Virginia and Maryland, farmers raised and marketed surplus wheat, corn, and rye, plus pork and beef. Some provisions were sold to rural craftsmen, but most food-stuffs went to towns and ports along the coast by wagon and by water transportation. Much grain and preserved meat passed directly into the holds of ships and moved to waiting markets overseas. Indeed, Carville Earle and Ronald Hoffman have argued that wheat farmers using wage labor during the harvest season earned greater profits than tobacco growers who relied on slave labor in many Chesapeake counties after 1750. In southern New England many farmers shifted largely out of grain crops and into animal husbandry. In Rhode Island, many landholders concentrated on raising horses for export to the Caribbean sugar plantations.

Generally speaking, the commercial aspects of agriculture were not as evident in the north as in the south, since by and large, farmers simply raised excess quantities of the same foodstuffs consumed in the household. This factor tends to obscure the market orientation of northern farmers, especially in the middle colonies.

This depiction of the colonial farmer as an individual who generally responded to price signals and opportunities in the marketplace has been questioned by James Henretta. In a recent article, he argued that communal values or lineal ties predominated over individualistic impulses in the northern colonies and that agricultural entrepreneurship was significantly stifled. In most northern counties, fathers held title to family lands long after their sons had reached maturity. The failure of these surplus sons to migrate to other areas where land was more abundant suggested to Henretta that the maintenance of kinship ties had a higher priority than personal material advancement. (Gregory Stiverson noted the same behavior pattern in his study of Maryland tenants.) In support of his hypothesis about the peculiar "mentalité" of colonial farmers, he cited the absence of crop specialization and the limited impact of foreign markets on northern agriculture.

The Henretta hypothesis tends to reinforce the argument of this book about the fundamentally static nature of economic life styles in colonial society. But whereas he stresses the importance of cultural values in restraining individualism and the pursuit of material advancement, most economic historians would probably place more emphasis on the slowness of technological change in colonial agriculture, especially the limitations imposed on productivity by bottlenecks in the harvesting of grains. Limited opportunities for entrepreneurship rather than public attitudes about the maintenance of lineal ties was the major inhibiting factor in my view. Moreover, in this case, and in so many other situations, the vantage point of the historian can make a critical difference in rendering judgment. Viewed from the twentieth century, colonial farmers may appear lethargic in responding to economic opportunities; but in comparison with their predecessors and contemporaries around the globe, it would probably be difficult to identify another class of family farmers who pursued so vigorously their own self-interest.

Finally the emphasis on communal values seems completely inappropriate for the colonial south. Kinship ties were not as tight in the south among the white population. Southern farmers exhibited obvious signs of entrepreneurial behavior in expanding the size of slave holdings to maximize profits. The southern colonies were also actively involved in foreign trade; by the late colonial period almost 50 percent of the region's total production—foodstuffs and staples—entered the export market. Many southern farmers were extensively committed to the commercial aspects of agriculture, while the remainder aspired to acquire the wherewithal to expand production.

The south was also distinctive because three major crops—tobacco, rice, and indigo—were unique to the region and two were not foodstuffs. The overall system of cultivation was quite different and thus requires further explanation. The southern colonies relied extensively, but not exclusively, on what had become by the eighteenth century a permanent system of black slave labor. In truth, the largest group of southern farmers owned no slaves at all, and within the slave-holding class, most farmers owned fewer than five slaves. Yet for the southern economic elite, the slave system permitted the creation of large agricultural units with work forces sometimes numbering over one hundred laborers.

Tobacco was a plant cultivated in many parts of the world prior to the seventeenth century, but it grew especially well in Chesapeake soils. The number of European consumers increased steadily after 1620, and they came to prefer the Virginia and Maryland leaf because of its texture, flavor, and relatively low price.

In the upper south, tobacco was the major cash crop throughout the colonial period. The typical Chesapeake farmer, with only his immediate family as a labor source, planted around 3 acres in tobacco, along with 10 to 15 acres in corn and other crops. Tobacco plants required close attention to obtain a quality leaf. The leaves were cut in late summer and hung in the tobacco barn to dry for three to six weeks. The leaf was then sorted according to grade and packed in hogsheads for shipment first to a downriver warehouse and later to England or Scotland. The average farm produced around 2,400 pounds of salable tobacco annually, and based on price levels after 1720, the family earned £10 to £20 ($650–$1300) for its efforts. Income from tobacco sales generated from 10 to 25 percent of a family's overall net income.

In the seventeenth century, tobacco was marketed almost exclusively under the consignment system. The grower retained ownership and assumed all risks throughout the marketing process, paying transportation and incidental costs until his crop was finally sold in England. The tobacco merchant negotiated the sale and charged a commission for his services, often 2.5 percent of the gross sales price plus the import duties, which amounted to almost 10 percent of the grower's net proceeds. The grower invariably sent along a list of finished goods for the return trip, and his English consignee had instructions to use the sale proceeds to fill that list. In supplying these finished goods, the merchant enjoyed either a handsome markup on items sold out of his stock or, at least, a second commission for purchasing the requested goods from other suppliers.

In addition, the merchant frequently offered "advances." He allowed growers to draw funds prior to the sale of the tobacco in Britain, with the understanding that the forthcoming crop served as collateral for the loan. Growers often used these advances to buy more land or new slaves. When the sale proceeds failed to cover the advance or the cost of ordered goods or both, many tobacco merchants agreed to extend credit to their colonial customers. Convenient credit terms were used to attract more consignments and to hold old accounts, and competitive pressures led tobacco merchants to adopt generally liberal policies.

Although the consignment system continued throughout the colonial era, aggressive Scottish merchants invaded the market after 1740 and inaugurated the practice of buying tobacco in the colonies for spot cash or its equivalent. Concentrating mainly on Virginia, the Glasgow merchants opened branch stores along the shores of the major rivers, where they exchanged tobacco for other merchandise. Like their competitors in London, the Scottish houses extended credit to growers in anticipation of the next season's crop.

The entrepreneurship of Glasgow tobacco merchants gave growers an alternative marketing channel, and they captured the lion's share of the business by the 1770s, especially within the ranks of the smaller farmers. The offer of spot cash appealed to many Chesapeake growers, because it eliminated the risks and uncertainties associated with later sale by a consignee in an overseas market. With poor communications, the news about prevailing prices in London was always weeks out-of-date and predictions about the future course of the tobacco market were unreliable. Moreover, the store managers paid prices for lower and medium grades that were competitive with the net proceeds normally realized in the London market.

The Glasgow merchants paid good prices partly because they operated with lower transportation costs. The westbound trip to the colonies from Scotland was often two or three weeks faster than from London because of differences in currents and winds. More important, the turnaround time in Virginia and Maryland was shorter. Vessels out of London servicing the consignment trade might spend several weeks in Chesapeake waters accumulating a full cargo for the return voyage. But the Scottish ships usually found a full cargo of hogsheads waiting at the firm's stores and ready for immediate loading. With transport costs reduced, the Glasgow tobacco merchants were in a position to offer higher prices to colonial growers. According to Jacob Price, tobacco transactions often resulted in only slight gains for the merchants or even small bookkeeping losses; the great profits in the Chesapeake trade actually came from the branch stores' sale of English and European goods to growers at substantial markups.

Despite the rise of the Glasgow contingent, some growers still preferred to deal with London commission merchants. Because of market fluctuations, the risk of loss was greater, but so too was the opportunity to realize higher tobacco prices and larger overall profits. Growers who produced premium grades of leaf, for instance in the York River region of Virginia, generally consigned their tobacco to the London market. Many large planters with big shipments and a willingness to accept greater risks also avoided sales to nearby stores and relied on the traditional consignment system. Yet such consignments probably accounted for no more than 20 percent of the total crop by the 1770s.

The organization of the marketing system for tobacco was one factor responsible for the lack of extensive urbanization in the upper south. Only two Chesapeake cities had populations over 5,000 as late as 1776; Norfolk and Baltimore each had around 6,000 inhabitants, and both were involved heavily in the West Indies trade and had few ties with tobacco. One reason for the absence of large commercial centers in the most populous colonial region was the excellent system of natural waterways. The broad rivers of Virginia, and many inlets of the Chesapeake Bay in Maryland, were navigable far inland, which permitted large ships to sail up to the wharves of individual planters. Larger growers often performed mercantile functions for smaller farmers nearby. Therefore, no central collection point for hogsheads was required at points along the Atlantic coast.

The concentration of merchandising functions in the hands of London, Glasgow, and other British tobacco merchants reinforced the decentralized character of the trade in the colonies and the rural structure of Chesapeake society. This concentration occurred because tobacco was an enumerated product and handling it in Britain involved complex procedures. Upon arrival, the importer was required to pay a heavy duty of from 200 to 300 percent ad valorem or, alternatively, to post bond. After a careful examination and grading of the tobacco, up to 85 percent was reexported to the continent, and the merchant was then permitted to collect a full drawback of the original import duties. Only British merchants had access to the credit and financial resources needed to expedite these tobacco transactions. The net result was that indigenous merchants played a minor role in the marketing system, and wherever tobacco was the major commercial crop, the growth of urban areas was severely arrested.

Despite the importance of tobacco in the Chesapeake economy, revenues from this staple represented no more than 10 to 20 percent of the typical family's annual income. Fluctuations in tobacco prices clearly had an impact on farm income, but they were not the sole indicator of the condition of the Chesapeake economy. For example, a bad harvest of food crops probably had a greater effect on farm income. A substantial decline of 30 percent in tobacco revenues reduced the typical family's yearly income from 3 to 6 percent, whereas a similar 30 percent shortfall in the harvest of food crops as a result of weather variations, or insect infestation, would have lowered income by as much as 15 percent.

Moreover, the effects of crop failures were much broader than declines in tobacco prices. Lower revenues from tobacco production had little impact on the living standards of slaves, who comprised almost 40 percent of the Chesapeake population by the 1770s. On the other hand, a sharp reduction in the yields of food crops was likely to translate into less variety in slave diets and smaller allotments of pork and beef. Only the great planters who depended on tobacco revenues to support their elevated life-style had a large stake in the maintenance of steady prices in the staple market. For the vast majority of the population—small farmers and slaves—the fluctuations in the harvest of food crops probably had a greater effect on real incomes than fluctuations in tobacco prices.

In the deep south, rice and indigo had emerged as the main commercial crops by the mid-eighteenth century. These semitropical plants thrived in the hot and humid lowlands along the coast of South Carolina and Georgia. Circumstantial evidence indicates that greater economies of scale existed in rice and indigo production than in tobacco, for much more of the deep south's output came from large plantations with numerous slaves. In South Carolina and Georgia the value of exports per capita, including slaves, was £3.65 ($237); for whites alone the figure was £8.88 ($577); which was by far the highest total in the colonies. The white residents of the deep south colonies had the best living standards on the mainland largely because of these huge earnings from overseas sales.

Indigo became a major commercial crop after the British Parliament authorized a bounty of 6 pence per pound for its production in 1748. The leaves of the indigo plant yielded a brilliant copper or purple dye which the English textile industry valued highly. Prior to the 1740s, the English cloth makers had purchased indigo mainly from the French and Spanish islands in the West Indies. After the Caribbean indigo plant was shown to adapt well to the mainland environment, Parliament, in sound mercantilist fashion, decided to subsidize its cultivation on British territory and thereby improve the empire's overall balance of trade. It is questionable whether indigo could have

been profitably grown in the lower south without the government sub-
sidy, since, after the political break with England in 1776 ended the
bounty, indigo cultivation rapidly declined and had almost disap-
peared by 1790.

Meanwhile, indigo production expanded rapidly in South Carolina
in the third quarter of the century. Like tobacco, it was produced almost exlusively for the export market. The indigo plants grew on high
ground unsuitable for rice paddies. The leaves were cut twice in summer on the mainland compared to up to four cuttings in the semitropical Indies. Extracting the dye residue from the leaves in large vats
on the plantation was a fairly complicated chemical process that determined in large part the quality and value of the final product. In
addition to raising enough food to feed his family, a skilled slave could
usually care for 2 acres of indigo plants and produce 120 pounds of
dye substance worth £20 to £30 ($1,300–$1,950) for the export
market in the early 1770s. Probably no other crop produced a greater
income per acre, or per worker, than indigo during the late colonial
period.

In terms of aggregate output, however, rice was the most important
crop in the deep south colonies. Along with corn, it was a mainstay in
local diets, and the land and workers were so productive that
enormous surpluses were available for overseas sale. Like wheat from
the middle colonies, rice found steady markets in the Caribbean sugar
islands and in both northern and southern Europe.

Rice was grown largely on plantations located in the swampy lowlands along the Atlantic coast. Slave labor was used extensively in
cultivating this commercial food crop. Two factors appear to have accounted principally for the slave character of rice agriculture. First, laborers working cooperatively in groups of five to ten were apparently
more efficient in growing rice in the field than the individual farmer
aided by his immediate family. Rice plantations were normally large
economic units and slave populations of 50 to 100 were common.
Indeed, South Carolina became the only colony where black slaves
outnumbered white inhabitants, and by a margin of 50 percent.

Another factor encouraging the use of slaves was the reputation of the coastal lowlands as an unhealthful region teeming with a host of mysterious fevers. Fearful whites often spent part of the year in Charleston hoping to escape the diseases associated with the swampy rice fields. For reasons inexplicable at the time, black workers seemed on the whole more immune to disease on rice plantations, and thus planters viewed blacks as better suited than whites to this form of agriculture.

Only in recent times have modern medical researchers discovered the probable biological explanation for this previously perplexing difference in the health pattern of the races. Although the chemical mechanism is still not fully understood, it has been fairly well established that individuals whose blood molecules reveal the so-called sickle-cell trait exhibit an unusually high degree of immunity to malaria. If husband and wife are both carriers of this trait, their children are vulnerable to the serious genetic disease called sickle-cell anemia. While members of other races in rare cases also possess the blood characteristic [the author is one], the incidence of sickled cells is concentrated in the descendants of black Africans. One hypothesis holds that through a process of Darwinian natural selection over thousands of years, persons with the sickle-cell mutation fared better in the malaria-infested regions of West Africa, and they gradually became a significant part of the general population. At present, approximately 10 percent of the the Afro-American population are carriers of the sickle-cell trait, and assuming a similar proportion of colonial slaves were carriers too, it follows that some blacks were less susceptible to chronic malaria than others and were, in fact, unusually healthy and productive workers in rice fields.

The strain of white rice widely grown in the lower south was not a native plant. Historians are unsure, however, about whether Europeans or Africans were most responsible for developing the technology of rice agriculture in South Carolina in the late seventeenth century. There is some doubt about how much exposure the white settlers who came to the mainland from the Caribbean sugar islands had had to rice growing, but many West Africans were already quite familiar with the techniques of dike building, flooding, weeding, and harvesting. Thus blacks may have taught their white masters more about the cultivation of this crop than vice versa.

Rice was a very profitable crop in the late colonial period. Yields were from 2 to 4 barrels per acre, and most plantations had 2 or 3 acres under cultivation for each field hand. Based on an average price of £2.3 ($150) per barrel from 1768 to 1772, slaves generated revenues annually of from £9.2 up to £27.6 ($600–$1,800), with around £15 ($975) probably the average figure, based on my analysis of trade data in the recent study by Shepherd and Walton.

In addition to an environment uniquely suited to growing certain semitropical crops, the southern colonies provided the setting for the emergence of a distinct economic and political elite—the planter class. The planter elite played a major role in the tobacco regions of the upper south, and it dominated the rice and indigo agriculture of South Carolina and Georgia. In North Carolina, wealthy planters were less numerous, yet they were still the most influential political force within the colony.

To rise in the social and economic order, a settler had to accumulate both land and slaves; and although no agreement exists among historians about the requirements for full planter status, by the time a man had acquired 500 acres and 20 slaves, he had clearly become an important member of the local society. Below the elite on the economic and social ladder were many aspiring settlers who owned a few slaves and who still worked in the fields performing the same tasks as their bondsmen. The great planters, who did no physical labor, but who supervised the work of others, provided the model for other ambitious whites to imitate.

The planter class held enormous political power in the southern colonies. The southern legislatures were composed largely of wealthy planters, who also filled most of the important judicial and administrative offices. Because of this planter dominance, the south mirrored more closely than the north the structure of society in the mother country. In England, the landed gentry remained the most potent force in governmental affairs.

Yet substantial differences existed between the English gentry and the colonial planter—in terms of the sources of political power and, more important to this study, the performance of economic functions. The colonial elite exercised governmental control with the active support of the general population. Unlike England, where the franchise was narrowly restricted, most farmers in the colonies were eligible to vote, and, in a very deferential manner, they normally elected wealthy neighbors who were well qualified to protect local interests. In the south, the great planters were the representatives of small farmers in public affairs.

In the scope of his economic activities, the colonial planter was likewise quite different from the English gentry. In the mother country, the gentry were primarily landlords who rented small farms to a large number of tenant families. Because his peers viewed nonagricultural pursuits as socially degrading, the English landlord refused to become extensively involved in mercantile activities.

The great planters in the mainland colonies were, in contrast, deeply involved not only in the management of their estates but simultaneously in a wide range of complementary enterprises. Few southerners achieved great wealth through agriculture alone; the great planters were simultaneously land developers, moneylenders, lawyers, and part-time merchants.

The planter class in the southern colonies was hardly isolated from the mundane world of business. Planters were generally active entrepreneurs who were inclined to engage in any form of economic activity that promised to pay an adequate return on the time and money invested. Most handled the business affairs and the record keeping for their own estates. In the absence of active commercial centers, southern planters typically performed a number of ancillary mercantile functions. Many planters became middlemen between neighboring farmers and established merchants in overseas ports. They bought small lots of tobacco from lesser neighbors and sold them, in return, finished goods imported from Britain. Occasionally, a planter loaned surplus funds to nearby friends or extended credit to small farmers.

One of the most prominent Virginia planters during the first half of the eighteenth century was William Byrd II, whose Westover plantation home above the James River remains one of that state's major architectural showcases. Our knowledge of Byrd's life style is unusually complete because he was a prolific writer and because his personal diary written in a secret code was deciphered and published in the twentieth century.

Byrd was full of paradoxes. In his Virginia habitat, he was an enormously wealthy man with thousands of acres of land and hundreds of slaves. He was a member of the upper chamber in the legislature and a powerful man in the political affairs of the colony. He accumulated a substantial library, hired European tutors to educate his children in intellectual and cultural matters, and kept up as best he could on current events at home, in England, and on the continent. In his own territory, he appeared at first glance to be almost the mirror image of a respectable member of the English gentry.

But when he went back to visit friends and relatives in the mother country, he was—like virtually every other colonial—not taken very seriously. In English society, "colonials," whether from North America, India, or any other location, were invariably viewed as pretentious upstarts. On a comparative basis, Byrd's wealth was barely middling; his political influence where it really counted—in England—was negligible; and his social position was inferior. Cultural refinement was virtually impossible from the British perspective, for Byrd lived literally thousands of miles from London and sophisticated society. Moreover, to accumulate and perpetuate his wealth, he relied on an unsavory slave system, and probably even more damning, he was actively involved, along with hired white overseers, in the management of his own fields and his black labor force. (British investors in sugar plantations in the Caribbean, which relied even more heavily on slavery, normally remained absentee owners and were thus less tarnished by their association with slave labor.) At home in Virginia he was a representative of the economic, political and social elite, but in Britain, Byrd—and his fellow colonial planters—had to struggle for even a semblance of recognition.

In an article discussing the role of market forces in the lives of William Byrd II and other great planters, Michael Greenberg describes the southern elite as a mix of aristocratic aspiration and bourgeois reality. Byrd aimed at economic success through competition in the marketplace while he attempted to create an aristocratic life-style. In his relationship with his black slave force, he was motivated both by paternalism (visiting the sick every day) and by unrestrained profit— two strategies which were by no means incompatible, as historians ranging from Robert Fogel and Stanley Engerman to Eugene Genovese have shown. The great southern planters combined traits of the refined gentry and of the calculating merchant. The links with modern, large-scale agriculture—commercial specialization for distant markets and heavy capital investments in men or machinery—can be traced back to the colonial planters.

A brief glance at the correspondence of William Fitzhugh, a Virginia tobacco grower and part-time lawyer who managed the family estate in the late seventeenth century, provides further insight into the economic status and life-style of the great planters. In a letter of April 1686, Fitzhugh described in great detail the extent of his holdings along the Potomac River in northern Virginia:

The Plantation where I now live contains a thousand Acres, at least 700 Acres of it being rich thicket, the remainder good hearty plantable land, . . . together with a choice crew of Negroes, . . . twenty-nine in all, with Stocks of cattle and hogs at each Quarter; upon the same land is my own Dwelling house, furnished with all accommodations for a comfortable and gentile living, . . . with 13 Rooms in it, . . . nine of them plentifully furnished with all things necessary and convenient, and all houses for use well furnished with brick Chimneys, four good Cellars, a Dairy, Dovecoat, Stable, Barn, Henhouse, Kitchen and all other conveniences, . . . a large Orchard of about 2500 apple trees most grafted, . . . a Garden a hundred foot square, . . . together with a good Stock of Cattle, hogs, horses, Mares, sheep and etc.

As Fitzhugh's description of his estate indicates, the economic position of the planter class was manifest primarily in the grandeur of the family residence and the elegance of its furnishings. A luxurious standard of living in this era was reflected in the finery of dress, the spaciousness of the home, the stylishness of the furniture, the craftsmanship in the silverware, and the convenience of having servants who performed routine household tasks.

In sum, the great strength of the colonial economy rested on its formidable agricultural base. The elegant life styles of the great planters derived from the production of a few staple crops in heavy demand overseas. Of even greater importance in this context, however, was the copious per capita production of more mundane crops, such as corn, wheat, and other grains, throughout the colonies. The regular surpluses of food crops supported a substantial population of livestock and gave the colonists a generally protein-rich diet. With over four-fifths of the population engaged primarily in agriculture, the extent of productivity on farms and plantations overshadowed completely the contributions of all other economic sectors to colonial living standards.

BIBLIOGRAPHICAL ESSAY

The best sources on colonial farming are the innovative studies of historical geographers. James Lemon, *The Best Poor Man's Country: A Geographical Study of Early Southeastern Pennsylvania* (Baltimore, Md.: Johns Hopkins University Press, 1972) is one outstanding book. Other valuable volumes in the same genre are Douglas McManis, *Colonial New England: A Historical Geography* (New York: Oxford University Press, 1975); Carville Earle, *The Evolution of a Tidewater Settlement System: All Hallow's Parish, 1650–1783*, Dept. of Geography Research Paper No. 170 (Chicago: University of Chicago, 1975); Robert D. Mitchell, *Commercialism and Frontier: Perspectives on the Early Shenandoah Valley* (Charlottesville: University Press of Virginia, 1977); and Roy Merrens, *Colonial North Carolina in the*

Eighteenth Century: A Study in Historical Geography (Chapel Hill: University of North Carolina Press, 1964).

For overviews of farming over longer periods, see two classics and two newer studies: Lewis Gray, *History of Agriculture in the Southern United States to 1860*, 2 vols. (Washington, D.C.: Carnegie Institute, 1933); Percy Bidwell and John Falconer, *History of Agriculture in the Northern United States, 1620–1860* (New York: Smith, 1941); John Schlebecker, *Whereby We Thrive: A History of American Farming, 1607–1972* (Ames: Iowa State University Press, 1975); and John Shover, *First Majority–Last Minority: The Transformation of Rural Life in America* (Dekalb: Northern Illinois University Press, 1976). Articles which touch on environmental issues are E. L. Jones, "Creative Disruptions in American Agriculture, 1620–1820," *Agricultural History* (October 1974), pp. 510–28, and Conway Zirkle, "To Plow or Not to Plow: Comment on the Planter's Problems," *ibid.* (January 1969), pp. 87–89. The relative prices of various grains in one urban market are listed in Karen Friedmann, "Victualling Colonial Boston," *ibid.* (July 1973), pp. 189–205.

On the issue of tenancy, these sources were valuable: Sung Bok Kin, *Landlord and Tenant in Colonial New York: Manorial Society, 1664–1775* (Chapel Hill: University of North Carolina Press, 1978); Gregory Stiverson, *Poverty in a Land of Plenty: Tenancy in Eighteenth-Century Maryland* (Baltimore, Johns Hopkins University Press, 1977); and Stephen Innes, "Land Tenancy and Social Order in Springfield, Massachusetts, 1652 to 1702," *William and Mary Quarterly* (January 1978), pp. 33–56. An analysis of the distribution of wealth is Jeffrey Williamson and Peter Lindert, "Long Term Trends in American Wealth Inequality," Institute for Research on Poverty, Discussion Paper No. 472–77 (Madison: University of Wisconsin, 1977).

On northern farming, I found especially useful Carl Bridenbaugh, *Fat Mutton and Liberty of Conscience in Rhode Island, 1636–1690* (Providence, R.I.: Brown University Press, 1974). The research on southern farmers and planters is fairly extensive. Thomas J.

Wertenbaker, *The Planters of Colonial Virgina* (Princeton, N.J.: Princeton University Press, 1922) is an older book that remains useful. Two new studies that focus on individual planters are Pierre Marambaud, *William Byrd of Westover, 1674–1744* (Charlottesville: University Press of Virginia, 1971) and Richard B. Davis, ed., *William Fitzhugh and His Chesapeake World, 1676–1701* (Chapel Hill: University of North Carolina Press, 1963). Good data on smaller farmers comes from Gregory Stiverson, "Early American Faming: A Comment," *Agricultural History* (January 1976), pp. 37–44; Edward Papenfuse, Jr., "Planter Behavior and Economic Opportunity in a Staple Economy," *ibid.* (April 1972), pp. 297–311; and D. Alan Williams, "The Small Farmer in Eighteenth-Century Virginia Politics," *ibid.* (January 1969), pp. 91–102.

Russell Menard has produced some solid figures on tobacco prices; see his "Farm Prices of Maryland Tobacco, 1659–1710," *Maryland Historical Magazine* (April 1973), pp. 80–85, and "A Note on Chesapeake Tobacco Prices, 1618–1660," *Virginia Magazine of History and Biography* (October 1976), pp. 401–10. For research on southern wheat production, see David Klingaman, "The Significance of Grain in the Development of the Tobacco Colonies," *Journal of Economic History* (June 1969), pp. 268–78, and Carville Earle and Ronald Hoffman, "Staple Crops and Urban Development in the Eighteenth-Century South," in Donald Fleming and Bernard Bailyn, eds., *Perspectives in American History,* (1976), 10:7–77.

For information on the marketing and financing of the tobacco crop, see Stuart Bruchey, *The Colonial Merchant: Sources and Readings* (New York: Harcourt, Brace & World, 1966); Warren Billings, ed., *The Old Dominion in the Seventeenth Century: A Documentary History of Virginia, 1606–1689* (Chapel Hill: University of North Carolina Press, 1975); and T. M. Devine, *The Tobacco Lords: A Study of the Tobacco Merchants of Glasgow and their Trading Activities, c1740–1790* (Edinburgh: John Donald, 1975). Over the years, numerous articles have appeared in the *William and Mary Quarterly*: Jacob Price, "The Rise of Glasgow in the Chesapeake Tobacco Trade, 1707-1775," (April 1954), pp. 179-99; Price, "Who was John Norton? A Note on the Historical Character of Some Eighteenth-Century London Virginia Firms," (July 1962), pp. 400-7; and Samuel Rosenblatt, "The Significance of Credit in the Tobacco Consignment Trade: A Study of John Norton & Sons, 1768-1775," (July 1962), pp. 383-99.

For coverage of the rice and indigo economies, see Lelia Sellers, *Charleston Business on the Eve of the American Revolution* (Chapel Hill: University of North Carolina Press, 1934); Peter Wood, *Black Majority: Negroes in Colonial South Carolina from 1670 through the Stono Rebellion* (New York: Knopf, 1974); and David Coon, "Eliza Lucas Pinckney and the Reintroduction of Indigo Culture in South Carolina," *Journal of Southern History* (February 1976), pp. 61-76.

An article stressing the familial ties of northern farmers is James Henretta, "Families and Farms: Mentalité in Pre-Industrial America," *William and Mary Quarterly* (January 1978), pp. 3-32. The conflict between aristocratic ambitions and commercial success in the south is examined in Michael Greenberg, "William Byrd II and the World of the Market," *Southern Studies* (Winter 1977), pp. 429-56.

CHAPTER IV

SERVANTS AND SLAVES

T
H E planters amassed great wealth primarily by exploiting
the labor of other human beings, black-skinned and white.
The degree of exploitation in the colonies varied according to
time and location. By the late colonial period, the rates of return on investments in bound labor were frequently reported as high as 20 to 30
percent in the rice- and indigo-growing regions of Georgia and South
Carolina, but were usually no higher than 10 to 15 percent in the
Chesapeake tobacco country and the northern colonies, and were
perhaps as low as 6 percent in some regions. These profits represented
the surplus which slaves and servants produced beyond the funds required to feed, clothe, house, and care for them, with the rate of return
calculated on the basis of the original purchase price or the sum invested in maintaining them during their unproductive childhood years.
Based on these profit levels, owners in the deep south often raised
their standard of living twofold after the acquisition of only three or
four bondsmen, whereas owners in the other colonies normally needed
a supplementary labor force of eight to ten bondsmen to achieve a
similar doubling in family income. In the southern colonies, wealth
and the extensive use of bound labor were virtually synonymous.

The rise of the plantation system coincided with the expanded use of
bound labor in the Chesapeake region after 1630. Manpower was the
scarcest resource in colonial America, and the opportunity to enlarge
the supply of labor through the acquisition of servants and slaves
proved irresistible. Vast estates were actually of only modest value
without complementary workers to develop the land, till the fields,
and harvest the crops.

Before 1680, when Virginia and then Maryland were undergoing
the early waves of settlement, the most common form of bound labor
was the white indentured servant. Indeed, from one-half to perhaps

two-thirds of those Englishmen who came to Virginia between 1630 and 1680 arrived in servile status. In return for the cost of a complete outfit of clothes, a steady diet, and transportation across the Atlantic, the servant signed a legal contract, or indenture, which permitted the sale of his or her labor to the highest bidder in the colonies for a period usually from four to seven years. Estimates of outfitting and transportation costs vary from £6 to £10 ($390–$650), or 40 to 70 percent of average annual incomes in the colonies. The labor contracts of servants sold for £9 to £15 ($585–$975), depending on the age, sex, and skills of the servant, and on the local demand for bound labor. The contract normally specified the conditions of work and stipulated that the servant was entitled to reasonably good treatment, including an adequate diet, a generous supply of alcohol (presumably only for males), sufficient clothing, and decent lodging.

Most contracts called for the payment of a sizable bonus, either in land or money, upon the successful completion of the labor term. This feature provided an incentive for servants to remain faithful workers throughout the indenture. In the seventeenth century, freedom dues gave thousands of indentured servants the opportunity to become members of the expanding southern middle class.

The institution of indentured servitude, a temporary status somewhere between slavery and freedom, was perfectly acceptable in colonial society. The system was modeled on the apprenticeship tradition in Europe, whereby adolescents bound themselves to an employer in return for an opportunity to learn the skills of a given trade. In the colonies, servants normally learned instead the techniques of American agriculture and the skills of farm management.

Servants made a good return cargo for vessels engaged in the tobacco trade. Most were young persons, the majority males, between the ages of 15 and 25. Although some servants were kidnapped in England and forcibly brought to the colonies, the vast majority entered into contracts voluntarily. Scholars are still debating the social origins of indentures; the most recent evidence indicates that they were drawn from a wide spectrum of English society and in fairly equal numbers from the ranks of farmers and artisans, unskilled laborers, and domestic servants. They were not extensively recruited from the ranks of the incompetent, the criminal element, or other social outcasts.

The lure was the potential benefits of a new life in an atmosphere where labor was in heavy demand and where the opportunity to acquire land, after a few years of servitude, was genuine. At home in England, the likelihood of eventually rising to the status of landowner was almost nil. Moreover, servants were actually selling only a claim on their surplus production, for in this era of relatively low per capita output, from 50 to 75 percent of the fruits of their labor was normally returned in the form of food, clothing, shelter, and freedom dues. Despite their servile status, the living standards of colonial indentures were probably not much, if at all, below what they had been accustomed to in the mother country. From an economic standpoint, their sacrifice was minimal.

The competitive features of the indenture market have been outlined in recent work by David Galenson and Robert Heavner. In analyzing a sample of nearly 3,000 extant contracts housed in London, Galenson found that the terms of a given contract were the result of negotiation between the potential immigrant and a host of merchant contractors. Workers who appeared likely to be the most productive—on the basis of such factors as knowledge of a valuable trade or more advanced age (above 25)—were in the best position to bargain for the shortest contracts and the highest freedom dues. Galenson listed literacy as a positive factor enhancing the servant's bargaining position, but Heavner's research on the Philadelphia market in the 1770s indicated that literacy did not increase the value of labor contracts. In Galenson's sample the literacy rate for men was almost 70 percent, which was considerably higher than for the English population as a whole. Just over one-half of the servants in his sample listed trades, with the percentage rising along with the age of the individual.

Another factor sometimes affecting the length of the indenture was the immigrant's selected destination. For example, youths under the age of twenty who chose the West Indies sugar islands, where the opportunities to acquire land were diminishing and the climate was less healthful, normally were able to bargain for shorter contracts than those youths headed for the mainland. In general, Galenson and Heavner argued that the variations in the indenture contracts were based on rational economic considerations.

In the tobacco colonies, planters constantly complained about the poor quality of servant labor. Masters invariably described their white indentures as lazy, ignorant, and alcoholic idlers, who were universally ungrateful, unruly, and irresponsible. In the eighteenth century, planters depicted their blacks slaves in virtually identical words, which suggests that the status of subservience alone could explain many of the contemptuous white attitudes toward black slaves in colonial America and for decades thereafter.

In addition to the use of corporal punishment, masters could go to court to enforce the terms of a labor contract. If a servant failed to perform assigned duties clearly within the scope of the indenture agreement, or attempted to flee, or when a female servant became pregnant by someone other than her employer, the master asked a judge to impose penalties. Whippings were often ordered for members of both sexes. The most serious penalty was an extension of a servant's contract for additional years; merely the threat of extension was usually sufficient to keep most servants in line.

At the same time, the indentured, unlike slaves, also had the option of taking a cruel and overbearing master to court for breach of contract. Servants typically asked judges to instruct masters to abide by the term of the indenture or, if serious injury had already occurred, to reduce the length of service.

After 1680 black slaves steadily replaced indentured servants as the primary source of bound labor in the southern colonies, and the subsequent inflow of the indentured in the eighteenth century went mainly to the middle colonies. The number of Englishmen departing for the mainland colonies declined sharply from 1690 to 1760, but Scotch-Irish and German migration rose substantially, especially into Pennsylvania. Many of the new arrivals were actually redemptioners, who brought their own clothing and supplies but had insufficient funds to pay the full price of a transatlantic passage. In these cases, the term of their labor contract was adjusted to correspond with the amount still due for transportation to the colonies. A fair number of German redemptioners came in family units and went into service that way.

Despite the continued functioning of the indenture system until the 1770s, the impact of these later servants on the colonial labor market, even in Pennsylvania, was never as great in the eighteenth century as it had been it the early settlement of Virginia and Maryland. By 1774, only 2 percent of the colonial population were indentured servants. The opportunities for upward economic and social mobility were also lessened for the indentured, although not necessarily for redemptioners, in the last half of the colonial era. This institution of voluntary temporary servitude, with transactions between all participants normally occurring in a free-market environment, was primarily a feature of the English colonial system in the western hemisphere. (The French employed the system on a limited scale and the Spanish not at all.) Meanwhile, the mere existence of a recognized class of Europeans living in a state of "quasi-slavery" probably made it much easier for the white majority to accept with so few reservations the permanent enslavement of another race with an entirely different culture.

After yeomen farmers, the second largest occupational group in colonial America were black slaves. They functioned mainly as field hands, house servants, and occasionally craftsmen. By 1770, blacks composed 21 percent of the colonial work force; in Virginia, Maryland, and North Carolina they numbered 320,000 and represented 38 percent of the population, while in South Carolina they outnumbered whites by roughly 50 percent. In the north, only New York with 12 percent of its population comprised of blacks had an appreciable number of slaves, and the vast majority were house servants. Most of the successful urban merchants in the north owned slaves; indeed slaveholding was one of the common characteristics of the elite classes, north and south.

The beginning of the shift from a reliance on indentured servants to a reliance on slaves in the tobacco colonies in the late seventeenth century followed from a combination of economic, political, and social factors. In Virginia, tensions between large property holders tied closely to the established government and a group of lesser rivals on the frontier, who gained the active support of a sizable number of discontents from the lower classes including numerous servants and ex-servants, finally led to Bacon's Rebellion in 1676. Once the king's representatives had reestablished control over the government, the colonial leadership realized the probable benefits of moving toward a permanent labor force of enslaved Africans, who had been deprived of all political and civil rights by 1660. In a recent book on colonial Virginia, Edmund Morgan has suggested that the creation of a large class of permanent slaves, easily distinguished by skin color, was one factor accounting for the surprisingly high degree of solidarity among all sectors of the white community. Indeed, the emergence of a cohesive, free society based on the subjugation of black slaves may explain, Morgan hypothesized, why so many wealthy planters in the colonies were surprisingly attracted by the radical concepts of republicanism and white equality in the eighteenth century.

Meanwhile, improving economic conditions in the mother country reduced the number of Englishmen willing to sign indenture contracts in order to reach the colonies. The continued expansion of tobacco fields therefore required the substitution of a new labor source. Black slavery was already a well-established institution in the Caribbean and other colonized areas of the western hemisphere. Thus imitation, not innovation, guided the course of mainland labor policy.

Finally, Russell Menard found that the price of permanent slaves, with lower yearly upkeep, was only 2 to 3 times higher than the cost of gaining the temporary services of indentures in the 1690s. The profit motive alone favored the substitution of black labor for white. In contrast to the declining supply of servants, the number of Africans available for purchase rose steadily up to the 1740s. The thirteen colonies were only a small fraction of the overall hemispheric slave market, for no more than 5 percent of the Africans forcibly transported across the Atlantic came to the English mainland.

The constant infusion of fresh supplies held down the market prices of slaves and made them competitive with servant contracts. Robert Paul Thomas and Richard Bean have recently demonstrated that every aspect of the African slave trade—from procurement, to transport, to distribution—was characterized by highly competitive markets, with a large number of active participants. Given an open-market structure, the average prices for slaves exceeded only modestly the average costs of delivery to the New World. A normal profit of 8 to 12 percent was probably the rule. The reports of phenomenally high profits by individuals in the slave trade, at one time a major theme in historical accounts of this era, were largely myth.

The final irony remains that the major beneficiaries of this barbaric system of forced African labor were the consumers of sugar and tobacco. These products had been luxuries in Europe prior to colonization, but they fell sharply in price and had become habitual necessities for the middle and even lower classes by the eighteenth century. As a result of the slave trade, Thomas and Bean sarcastically observed, European consumers found "dental decay and lung cancer" available at bargain prices.

In a subsequent research project, Thomas and Bean offered an explanation for the timing of the shift from servants to slaves in the Chesapeake region. Plantations in the Caribbean area began the shift in the 1640s, but on the mainland the transition did not come until almost half a century later. First, they found no evidence that black slaves were inherently more productive in raising any specific crop, such as sugar or tobacco, or in working on large economic units. For them, the key to understanding lay in the relative prices of slaves and servants in the two markets.

The West Indies shifted to slavery in the 1640s because the price of Africans fell sharply while the contractual terms necessary to attract English servants became more costly. By the 1640s, most of the arable land on the British Caribbean islands was already occupied, and they offered diminishing opportunities to white immigrants. Meanwhile, economic conditions in England had improved and the difficulty in recruiting indentured servants on favorable terms was greater.

The Chesapeake region did not shift to slavery at this same point in time, according to Thomas and Bean, because labor prices in this market continued to favor servants. The net cost of transporting slaves (operating expenses plus mortality rates) remained £3 to £4 ($195–$260) higher to the mainland colonies than to the Caribbean. In addition, the contractual terms necessary to attract servants to the Chesapeake, which had a reputation for a more healthful climate and plentiful opportunities to acquire land, were still beneficial to planters.

In the 1680s and 1690s, wages in England rose again, and greater inducements were necessary to lure indentured servants. At the same time, the opening up of North Carolina and Pennsylvania to settlement raised the costs of enforcing indenture contracts, for the lure of inexpensive land and the improved chances of evading capture in combination encouraged servants to escape. Slave prices did not rise and the costs of preventing successful escapes remained low. By the 1690s, the cost of slaves was lower than for white servants on the mainland.

By the eighteenth century, planters found investments in slave labor more profitable than investments in servants. Ralph Gray and Betty Wood examined the transition to slavery in Georgia in the 1740s and discovered substantial differences in yearly expenses. The Georgia trustees estimated the annual cost of upkeep for a male servant at £9 ($585) compared to only £3.46 ($225) for a slave (table 4.1).

A close analysis of the data reveals, however, that three items—meat, cheese, and beer—accounted for almost all of the disparity in maintenance costs between servants and slaves. The allotments of basic foodstuffs and clothing were virtually identical. An English servant expected a liberal 200 pound allowance of beef and pork, or seven times the amount alloted for blacks. But remarkably, alcohol consumption accounted for a full 60 percent of the estimated differential; indeed beer rations were 37 percent of the estimated expenses for maintaining indentured servants. The cost of supplying servants with alcohol alone was just a shade below the food and cloth-

TABLE 4.1. Yearly Maintenance Costs For Servants and Slaves—
Georgia in the 1740s

Item	Servant		Slave	
	Amount	Cost	Amount	Cost
Rice	114 lbs.	£ .26	114 lbs.	£ .26
Peas	114 lbs.	.17	114 lbs.	.17
Flour	114 lbs.	.50	114 lbs.	.50
Basic Foodstuffs		£ .93		£ .93
Meat	200 lbs.	£1.67	30 lbs.	£ .25
Corn	—	—	13 bu.	.98
Beer		3.39	—	—
Cheese	18 lbs.	.60	—	—
Butter	9 lbs.	.36	—	—
Sugar		.23	—	—
Soap		.40	—	—
Clothing		1.42		1.30
Total		£9.00		£3.46

SOURCE: Ralph Gray and Betty Wood, "The Transition from Indentured to Involuntary Servitude in Colonial Georgia," *Explorations in Economic History* (October 1976), 13:353–70.

ing requirements of slaves. Despite the much smaller sums expended on slaves, it is questionable whether the overall combination of food and clothing left them with living standards in Georgia that much inferior to white servants. To the extent that the absence of gallons of beer from the yearly allotment protected a laborer from the potentially debilitating effects of alcoholism, which was a genuine threat in colonial America, a slave was in some cases perhaps better off with less.

Because the economy was overwhelmingly agricultural, slaves performed most of the same labor tasks as white, family farmers. The skill level of white and black farm workers was roughly the same. Slaves cleared land, prepared the soil for planting, tended the fields, and harvested the crops. Rice farming in the deep south was almost exclusively performed by slaves, however. On some large plantations slaves labored throughout the day in work gangs, but on other estates they received permission to halt work in the afternoon upon accomplishing an assigned task. Not only men but many black women were regular field hands; indeed the high participation rate of slaves of both sexes, young and old, in the labor force explains in part the economic viability of the slave system. Owners also tried to keep blacks active on a year-round basis. Slaveholders had a fixed investment in a human machine, and in an effort to minimize downtime, they tried to plan work schedules so that during the winter months blacks were kept busy mending fences, removing stumps, and performing other productive tasks.

According to a new study on the evolution of slave society in the Chesapeake region by Allan Kulikoff, the productivity of bonded labor rose over the course of the eighteenth century because of the decreasing percentage of untrained and unacclimated Africans in the black population. By 1740, only 17 percent of adult blacks in Virginia had arrived in the colony within the last decade. By the 1770s, the sex ratio was generally in balance, whereas early in the century males had outnumbered females by 50 percent.

The rising numbers of native-born slaves and the more balanced sex ratio were two factors leading to the emergence of an identifiable Afro-American culture. Early in the eighteenth century, most slaves had lived on small plantations and were isolated from contact with other blacks. Over the century the size of plantations increased, however, and provided the environment for the development of a settled community and a unique black culture. Unlike the vast majority of whites who lived on separate farms, many slaves increasingly lived in a small-village setting. Houses in the slave quarters were furnished with straw bedding, barrels for seating, a few pots and pans for cooking, and a grindstone or millstone for converting corn to meal. Kulikoff argues that after mid-century, the more concentrated pattern of black settlement, in comparison with the dispersed nature of the white population, resulted in the more advanced development of kinship ties among blacks.

One question which has perennially emerged in discussions of colonial agriculture is why slave labor was confined almost exclusively to the production of southern crops, such as tobacco, rice, and indigo. No laws or customs discouraged the purchase and use of slaves in the northern colonies. Except for a very small number of Quakers in the middle colonies, few whites recognized slavery as a serious moral issue. Instead it was strictly a matter of economics; where slavery proved profitable whites adopted it, and where it proved too costly they avoided it. Slavery was not used extensively in northern agriculture because it was unprofitable in regions which relied exclusively on the production of wheat and other grain crops.

An analysis of the northern Chesapeake, where wheat and tobacco were both grown, reveals sharp differences in labor requirements. Carville Earle and Ronald Hoffman found that although the two crops demanded about the same amount of aggregate labor to produce comparable output, the timing of the application of that labor varied significantly. Tobacco required constant attention during the growing season, but often the time consumed was only a few hours per day. Free white laborers customarily expected wages for an entire day, not a fraction thereof. Consequently, the hiring of free labor to tend tobacco fields was prohibitively expensive. Wheat, in contrast, was labor intensive only during the planting and harvest seasons and needed little care during the interim. Workers hired at the beginning and end of the grain cycle were fully utilized from sunup to sundown. Earle and Hoffman noted that even those wheat farmers who owned slaves still found it profitable to hire supplementary free labor during the harvest season. Because of the differentials in the timing of labor inputs, wheat farmers beyond the tobacco-growing regions of Virginia and Maryland generally found slave ownership less profitable than the reliance upon free labor. This factor explains why slavery, with the exception of house servants, failed to expand to the northern colonies.

A historian need not be an apologist for the slave system to argue that from a strictly economic standpoint, mainland blacks had an enviable standard of living compared to agricultural workers in most other parts of the world, including Africa and South America. Moreover, neither lengthy investigation nor complex quantification are necessary to justify this sweeping generalization; the evidence is implicit in the demographic data. The rate of natural increase for the black population was high by any standard of measurement.

Slaves on the mainland rarely feared economic deprivation. Like their masters, they had access to sizable plots of productive land for the cultivation of food crops. Meat and fish, while not plentiful, were normally a regular feature of slave diets on at least a weekly basis— which could not be said of most of the planet's inhabitants at the time. The overall health of blacks who were acclimated to North America was also relatively good. True, slaves missed out on most of the luxuries of this affluent pre-industrial society, such as a varied wardrobe, a large quota of meat, gallons of beer and rum, and more leisure time; but the basic necessities of life in terms of diet, clothing, and shelter were not lacking and indeed were quite liberal by contemporary world standards.

Unlike whites, however, slaves had no opportunity to reap additional benefits from their own productivity. They had no hope of acquiring land and improving their economic or social status, irrespective of individual effort. In sum, the second largest occupational group in North America contributed greatly to the exceptional prosperity of the colonies, yet they had permanent limitations placed on their participation in its material rewards.

BIBLIOGRAPHICAL ESSAY

For information on indentured servants, the starting point is Abbot E. Smith, *Colonists in Bondage: White Servitude and Convict Labor in America, 1607–1776*. (Chapel Hill: University of North Carolina Press, 1947). Russell Menard has examined the tobacco region in "Immigration to the Chesapeake Colonies in the Seventeenth Century: A Review Essay," *Maryland Historical Magazine* (Fall 1973), pp. 323–29, and in "From Servant to Freeholder: Status Mobility and Property Accumulation in Seventeenth-Century Maryland," *William and Mary Quarterly* (January 1973), pp. 37–64.

Robert Heavner covers one of the middle colonies in the eighteenth century in *Economic Aspects of Indentured Servitude in Colonial Pennsylvania, 1771–1773* (New York: Arno Press, 1977) and "Indentured Servitude: The Philadelphia Market, 1771–1773," *Journal of Economic History* (September 1978), pp. 701–13. On the social origins of indentures, see Mildred Campbell, "Social Origins of Some Early Americans," in James M. Smith, ed., *Seventeenth Century America: Essays in Colonial History* (Chapel Hill: University of North Carolina Press, 1959), pp. 63–89; David Galenson, "Middling People or 'Common Sort'?: The Social Origins of Some Early Americans Reexamined," with a rebuttal by Mildred Campbell, *William and Mary Quarterly* (July 1978), pp. 499–540; and Galenson, "The Social Origins of Some Early Americans: Rejoinder," with a reply by Campbell, *ibid.* (April 1979), pp. 264–286. The functioning of the indenture market in England is discussed in Galenson, "British Servants and the Colonial Indenture System in the Eighteenth Century," *Journal of Southern History* (February 1978), pp. 41–66, and "Immigration and the Colonial Labor System: An Analysis of the Length of Indenture," *Explorations in Economic History* (1977), 14:360–377.

Two books that discuss the transition from servants to slaves are Edmund S. Morgan, *American Slavery—American Freedom: The Ordeal of Colonial Virginia* (New York: Norton, 1975), and John Rainbolt, *From Prescription to Persuasion: Manipulation of Seventeenth-Century Virginia* (Port Washington, N.Y.: Kennikat Press, 1974). For an account of the transition in the lower south, see Ralph Gray and Betty Wood, "The Transition from Indentured to Involuntary Servitude in Colonial Georgia," *Explorations in Economic History* (October 1976), pp. 353–370.

Our knowledge of slave conditions comes primarily from studies focusing mainly on the first half of the nineteenth century: U. B. Phillips, *American Negro Slavery* (New York: Appleton, 1918); Kenneth Stampp, *The Peculiar Institution* (New York: Vintage, 1956); and Robert Fogel and Stanley Engerman, *Time on the Cross* (Boston: Little, Brown, 1974). Strong rebuttals to the controversial thesis of the latter book are found in the Paul David et al., eds., *Reckoning with Slavery* (New York: Oxford University Press, 1976).

Four articles surveying the Chesapeake region are T. H. Breen, "A Changing Labor Force and Race Relations in Virginia, 1660–1710," *Journal of Social History* (Fall 1973), pp. 3–25; Russell Menard, "Maryland Slave Population 1658 to 1730: A Demographic Profile of Blacks in Four Counties," *William and Mary Quarterly* (January 1975), pp. 29–54; Menard, "From Servants to Slaves: The Transformation of the Chesapeake Labor System," *Southern Studies* (Winter 1977), pp. 355–90; and Allan Kulikoff, "The Origins of Afro-American Society in Tidewater Maryland and Virginia, 1700 to 1790," *William and Mary Quarterly* (April 1978), pp. 226–59. An excellent book on slaves in the rice region is Peter Wood, *Black Majority: Negroes in Colonial South Carolina from 1670 through the Stono Rebellion* (New York: Knopf, 1974).

Two important studies by Robert Paul Thomas and Richard Bean are "The Fishers of Men: The Profits of the Slave Trade," *Journal of Economic History* (December 1974), pp. 885–914, and "The Adoption of Slave Labor in British America," in Henry Gemery and Jan Hogendorn, eds., *The Uncommon Market: Essays in the Economic History of the Atlantic Slave Trade* (New York: Academic Press, 1978), pp. 377–98.

For a survey of the recent scholarship on colonial slavery, see Peter Wood, "'I Did the Best I Could for My Day': The Study of Early Black History during the Second Reconstruction, 1960 to 1976," *William and Mary Quarterly* (April 1979), pp. 185–226. An article which came to my attention too late for inclusion in the text but which promises to improve substantially our understanding of colonial slavery is Ira Berlin, "Time, Space, and the Evolution of Afro-American Society on British Mainland North America" *American Historical Review,* in press.

CHAPTER V

ARTISANS AND MERCHANTS

A R T I S A N S and merchants comprised from 10 to 12 percent of the white occupational group. Although widely distributed throughout the economy, they tended to congregate in villages, towns, and port cities. Since there was little manufacturing in the colonial era, urban areas were almost entirely commercial and handicraft centers, populated by merchants, artisans, and common laborers. The merchant was the colonial businessman, and the term was loosely applied to individuals from poor storekeepers on the frontier to wealthy shipowners in the major ports. Artisan was likewise a category that cut a broad swath; it encompassed trades requiring minimal skills such as coopers, tailors, cordwainers (shoemakers), and weavers as well as elite craftsmen like silversmiths and instrument makers. At the bottom of urban society were unskilled laborers, about whom little is currently known.

Artisans were an important segment of the labor force in the colonies. Working largely with wood, leather, and metal materials, these skilled and semiskilled workers provided specialized services for the local community and sometimes engaged in small-scale production for limited markets. With the exception of hats and later shoes, few products were made for the export market.

Estimating the number of persons performing skilled work is difficult, however, because many farmers and their families participated in this labor market on a part-time or seasonal basis. Women were frequently involved in crude textile production in the home. Slaves occasionally acquired artisan skills too. Conversely, many artisans in villages and towns cultivated a few acres of farmland near their home or workplace. In this book, artisans are defined broadly as men who worked with their hands and earned over 50 percent of their income from nonfarm pursuits. They headed from 7 to 10 percent of colonial households.

The wages of artisans in the colonies were generally high. The demand for skilled labor grew more rapidly than the supply of able workers, and the chronic shortage held up wage rates. In England and continental Europe, workers had banded together into associations called guilds that, by restricting entry into a craft and through various licensing agreements, acted to limit artificially the supply of skilled labor. (The American Medical Association has employed similar techniques successfully in the twentieth century.) In the colonies, no artificial market restraints were required to maintain high wages, and the guild system was never permanently established. Contemporary sources put colonial wages at 30 to 100 percent above those paid for identical work in England.

The successful colonial artisan was typically an independent, self-employed worker who owned his own tools and furnished his own materials. His work was performed in the home or on the job. On occasion two or more craftsmen joined together to create a small shop. From one perspective, the artisan was also a small businessman, for he usually had a sizable investment in equipment and tools, managed his own work schedule, and kept his own accounts. Most artisans owned sufficient property to qualify as voters in municipal and provincial elections.

Craftsmen often took on apprentices as helpers and trainees. In the European tradition, the apprentice's parents normally paid the artisan a fee for agreeing to assume responsibility for teaching their son a marketable skill. A contract, similar to an indenture, was negotiated between the parties, which called upon the artisan to feed and house the youth and to teach him the skills of a useful trade in return for labor services. Many contracts terminated when the apprentice reached the age of twenty-one. Benjamin Franklin was one famous colonist who began his career as an apprentice in a print shop.

The range of nonfarm occupations in the colonies was wide and varied. The largest number of skilled and semiskilled workers were found in the towns and cities, where in response to larger markets, the greatest degree of specialization also existed. In a study of

Germantown, Pennsylvania, which lay five miles northwest of Philadelphia, Stephanie Wolf used tax records to compile a list of occupational categories in 1773, when the town's population was approximately 2,200. While not inclusive, the Germantown data provide a fairly representative sample of colonial craft and service occupations (table 5.1).

Some urban areas attracted a concentration of specialized workers. In Pennsylvania, the town of Lancaster had attracted larged numbers of weavers in the woolen and linen trades plus many gunsmiths by the late colonial period. Lynn, Massachusetts, became a center for shoe production, which was generally a cooperative family enterprise. Under

TABLE 5.1.   Artisan Occupations Listed by Germantown, Pennsylvania, Taxpayers in 1773

	No. workers		No. workers
Fabric crafts		*General crafts*	
Stocking weaver	20	*and industries*	
Weaver	11	Clockmaker	5
Tailor	12	Bookbinder	3
Hatter	6	Painter	3
Dyer	4	Printer	2
Leather crafts		*Woodworking*	
Cordwainer	17	*and building crafts*	
Tanner	10	Cooper	26
Saddlemaker	8	Mason	10
Skinner	7	Carpenter	9
		Joiner	8
Food production			
Butcher	10	*Transportation*	
Miller	6	*and services*	
Baker	4	Coachmaker	8
		Carter	8
Metal crafts		Wheelwright	6
Blacksmith	11		

SOURCE: Stephanie Grauman Wolfe, *Urban Village: Population, Community, and Family Structure in Germantown, Pennsylvania, 1693–1800* (Princeton, N.J.: Princeton University Press, 1976), pp. 106–7, table 10.

the domestic or putting-out system, merchant-entrepreneurs organized production, financed the inventory of materials, and provided outside markets. The shoemaker and his family periodically received payment for finished shoes on a piecework basis. Blanche Hazard credited Lynn with the production of approximately 80,000 pairs of shoes for domestic and foreign markets in 1768.

In port towns the shipping trade attracted a host of skilled workmen and mariners. In Philadelphia, where occupational data from the tax rolls of 1774 has survived, mariners comprised 9 percent of the identifiable workers; among them were 83 ship captains, 22 pilots, and 199 general seamen. Members of the shipbuilding and fitting-out crafts made up another 5 percent of the city's labor force. These men were ship carpenters, ropemakers, sailmakers, caulkers, joiners, and the like.

Shipbuilding in colonial America was in the hands of individual shipwrights, who operated small yards with few, if any, permanent employees. Working largely under contracts from merchants at home or abroad, a builder rarely produced more than two ships a year, although the pace of work in the colonies was generally considered much faster than in England. The work was seasonal, with little activity during the winter months.

Because of labor efficencies and lower material costs, especially timber, colonial ships were built at prices £2 to £4 ($130–$260) less per ton than in England. By the late colonial era, slightly over one half of all ship sales were to buyers in Britain and other parts of the empire. By that date, perhaps one-third of all British-owned ships had been built in colonial shipyards.

In addition to drawing up the building plans, the shipwright organized and coordinated the work of other craftsmen. At different stages of construction, he hired skilled artisans to perform specific tasks. No more than 10 to 15 workers were normally in the shipyard at any given time. The daily wages of these craftsmen were generally high, but irregular employment patterns and the seasonal nature of construction prevented them from earning yearly incomes much above those of other skilled artisans.

Although the largest concentrations of craftsmen lived in urban areas, others were scattered throughtout the countryside. Millers who ground grain into flour were virtually everywhere. In districts remote from trading centers, a versatile artisan with skills in several crafts could earn a modest living. Many became itinerant workers. In Granville County, North Carolina, which was located 150 miles inland from the Atlantic coast, Carl Bridenbaugh counted at least 41 craftmen between 1749 and 1776, including numerous carpenters, joiners, blacksmiths, wheelwrights, coopers, a haberdasher, a weaver, a tailor, a bricklayer, and a silversmith. Similarly, James Lemon found that about 20 percent of the taxpayers in rural Lancaster County, Pennsylvania, listed artisan occupations in 1759. Yet, except for millers, their economic and social status was below that of farmers, primarily because most owned no land.

Paralleling the experience of other occupational groups in colonial North America, the artisan's life style changed little over the decades. Technological change was slow. The products of farm and forest were fashioned by hand, using simple tools and traditional processes. The artisan was normally self-employed and independent, and he enjoyed the pride of craftsmanship which is absent so often in modern industrial societies.

In the major port cities, artisans held a middle rank in the community between the dominant merchant class and the "lower orders," composed of propertyless day laborers and seamen. Although merchants retained most of the important public offices, many artisans qualified as voters and were sometimes active in political affairs. In the last two decades before the war with Britain, artisans increasingly participated in the independence movement. They served often on the extralegal citizens committees formed to implement and enforce various nonimportation agreements aimed at British goods after 1765.

Artisans and merchants split frequently into opposing camps over the continuance of the trade boycotts which were periodically implemented to pressure Parliament to rescind legislation calling for increases in imperial taxes. After the first few months of a given boycott, those merchants who relied upon sales of British imports faced difficult times, because they were unable to replenish inventories. As time passed, these merchants normally pressed for modifications in the nonimportation agreements or their outright abandonment. Other merchants who were associated primarily with the West Indies trade rather than British imports were not greatly affected by the boycotts, and they tended to support them.

Meanwhile, artisans prospered from the boycott of British finished goods. In the absence of foreign competition, they generally expanded the volume and range of their business activities and reaped the benefits of higher prices for their products. Given these circumstances, it is easy to understand why the artisan class participated so willingly and so enthusiastically in the various efforts to punish the British through the tactic of the trade boycott.

During the last fifteen years, scholarly research has focused much more extensively on the economic, political, and social role of both artisans and common laborers in colonial society. Indeed, a number of historians have been actively examining the hypothesis that social and economic tensions within the major port cities contributed significantly to the revolutionary spirit and the independence movement. The list of scholars includes Gary B. Nash, Charles Olton, Eric Foner, Dirk Hoerder, and others. Their focus is primarily on the allegedly mounting dissatisfaction of the middle and lower classes with the distribution of wealth and property, which was skewed heavily in favor of the merchant class, and such issues as the rising cost of living, increased incidences of poverty and unemployment, higher domestic taxes, and imprisonment for debts.

Although it is too soon to assess the impact of this new research on historical interpretations of political events in the 1760s and 1770s, one fact remains indisputable: the artisan class played a much larger role in the public affairs of the thirteen colonies than their counterparts in any other society around the globe. From a comparative perspective, their economic, social, and political status was unrivaled anywhere. The same claim can be made—and even more emphatically—for the colonial merchant class.

The mercantile community was geographically dispersed throughout the thirteen colonies. Merchants coordinated the flow of trade between farm and town and with overseas markets. The mercantile network extended from the major cities through the towns and villages and out to the frontier. What usually linked together these disparate businesses was the extension of credit on sales and inventories. Credit was the tie that united the mercantile community and gave merchants similar views on the enforcement of contracts and the repayment of debts.

The scale of operations reflected the volume of transactions in a given area. On the frontier and in other remote rural regions, merchants were little more than country storekeepers. Some conducted business out of one room in their dwelling, while simultaneously maintaining a small farm. Despite his place on the lower rung of the mercantile ladder, the country storekeeper provided a number of critical services for the local economy. He was normally the only source of goods from the outside world, whether 50 or 3,000 miles away; he provided the only market for local farm surpluses; and he functioned as the most reliable source of credit for small farmers. In the more active trading centers, the volume of business was sufficient to support full-time merchants. They were the intermediaries in the mercantile chain, buying in bigger lots from other merchants in larger towns and port cities and selling a few items to numerous storekeepers in outlying regions.

Colonial business was a small-scale and highly personal form of economic activity. Mercantile firms were organized as proprietorships or partnerships, often with close relatives; the owners typically managed the daily operations of their enterprises. All business was conducted out of one location, and the pace of transactions was slow by modern standards—sometimes only two or three sales a day. The number of employees in even the largest mercantile houses were few— besides the partners, perhaps one or two men acted as clerks, stock boys, and bookkeepers.

The successful colonial merchant rarely specialized in any single line of goods but handled a wide range of merchandise. Since he often accepted payment in kind when customers were short of coin or paper currency, a merchant naturally acquired a variety of items in the course of selling his existing inventory. Most items fell within the classifications of food, spices, alcohol, textiles, hardware, and general household goods. He sold goods at retail prices to local customers and simultaneously acted as a wholesaler in relations with other merchants in outlying communities.

Because of the seasonal pattern of the predominantly agricultural economy, the merchant usually found that he had to extend credit terms of from three to nine months in order to maintain sales volume between harvests. He, in turn, required liberal credit terms from distant suppliers; long chains of credit were standard practice within the mercantile community. The original source of much outstanding credit in the colonies could be traced back to British merchants and their bankers. In England, capital was more plentiful, a condition which was reflected in the marketplace through lower interest rates and lenient credit terms.

In the major port cities, the leading merchants were engaged extensively in foreign commerce. Most mercantile fortunes were the result of profits in overseas ventures. An important merchant probably owned a few ships outright and almost certainly took fractional interests of, for example, one-third, one-fifth, or one-eighth in other ships and their cargoes. It was not unusual for the value of the cargo to exceed the cost of the vessel. Spreading risks through the device of fractional interests was an early substitute for marine insurance. If one ship went down at sea, the loss would not fall completely on the shoulders of a single merchant and threaten him with bankruptcy and ruin.

The established merchant rarely traveled overseas with his cargo. Sometimes he made prior arrangements with other merchants in distant ports to act as agents in his behalf on a commission basis. Under these agreements, goods were consigned to commission merchants, who handled foreign transactions for a negotiated percentage of the sales price, somewhere from 3 to 10 percent. But it was often difficult to establish business contacts with foreign merchants who were reliable and trustworthy, which explains why so much overseas commerce was conducted between relatives by blood or marriage. On other occasions, merchants designated the ship captain to handle business affairs in the foreign port. In situations where the captain was a poor businessman, merchants could send out an additional passenger called a supercargo, who was authorized to take care of business matters.

Commerce across long distances was inherently a risky proposition. Because communications were slow, information about conditions in overseas markets was invariably weeks or months out of date. Meanwhile, interruptions in the regular flow of trade caused the prices of commodities to fluctuate sharply. Merchants sending out goods to a foreign market on the basis of a rumored shortage often discovered that others, either by luck or greater enterprise, had already satisfied the local demand. As a precautionary measure, merchants sometimes instructed ship captains and supercargoes to sail for other nearby ports, especially around the Caribbean area, if prices for the outbound cargo were unusually depressed in the first market. The most successful merchants gave their overseas representatives instructions that contained a reasonable balance of guidance and flexibility about prices and routes.

A fine example of the wide-ranging activities of colonial merchants is provided by the Brown family of Providence, Rhode Island. James Hedges has written expertly about this prominent New England family, which later donated funds for the establishment of the venerable Brown University. Although the family had settled in Rhode Island in the 1640s, its fortunes improved dramatically in the 1720s after James Brown married the daughter of one of Providence's leading shipowners. James was made captain of one of his father-in-law's vessels, and he gained business experience on trips to the Caribbean, where provisions such as grain, horses, cheese, tar, and lumber were exchanged for molasses and rum.

In 1728, James Brown settled down to become a resident merchant in his own right. The trade with the sugar islands continued, and his brother Obadiah, after serving as supercargo on several voyages, joined the firm. In later decades, the family partnership began the direct importation of hardware, textiles, and other finished goods from England. Much of this merchandise was resold to inland store-keepers at markups of 60 to 75 percent, with four months credit at 6 percent interest.

For a short time, the Browns became involved in the slave trade. The partners financed three voyages to Africa in the 1760s—one ship was lost at sea, a second lost money after suffering many deaths in passage, and a third trip returned a small profit. After this third voyage, the family ceased its participation in the slave trade until one last voyage was undertaken late in the century. The absence of profits was surely one factor but moral considerations may have played a role as well, for Moses Brown eventually became a leading abolitionist and a sponsor of legislation curbing the slave trade in Rhode Island.

Beyond their regular commercial activities, the Browns also became investors in a series of manufacturing enterprises. These ancillary ven-tures were usually closely connected with their merchandising busi-ness. For example, one motive for building a small slaughterhouse was to provide a steady source of salted pork and beef for the outbound voyage to the sugar islands. Similarly, the family opened a rum distillery to process molasses and sugar imported from the Caribbean.

In the 1750s, the family built a small factory to produce high-quality candles from the head matter of sperm whales. The Browns' own vessels supplied some of the head matter for the spermaceti candles, but most of the pure white oil came from other whalers. The partners' candles quickly established a solid reputation in the New York and Philadelphia markets. To promote consumer identification with their product and increase sales, the Browns adopted the strategy of affixing the family's label to every box of candles shipped to out-of-town agents. This practice of putting a brand label on an item produced in bulk was uncommon, since most goods were then sold on the basis of their generic names.

The Browns extended their investments into iron production in the 1760s. In this venture, the family initially took a one-half interest in a new partnership with four other Rhode Island businessmen. Three of them withdrew after two years, and the family assumed almost complete control. The Browns were optimistic about the profit potential in iron because demand was strong both at home and in England, and because they had already developed close ties with commission merchants in New York and other cities through which the output could be marketed.

The furnace constructed near the village of Hope on the Pawtuxet River shared many characteristics with iron plantations in other colonies. The site was rural, since the ore, adequate supplies of wood for conversion into charcoal, and water power were all required at a common location. It was impractical to move either the ore or fuel any more than a few miles, because prior to the building of canals and railroads in the nineteenth century, overland transportation costs were prohibitive. Iron plantations in eastern Pennsylvania the center of the colonial industry, were usually situated in remote, heavily wooded locations. The Hope site was, however, near Providence in an area long settled and partially cleared. Therefore, the partners arranged contracts with local farmers in order to gain access to timber stands in the surrounding area.

In comparison with other colonial enterprises, iron production was a large-scale operation. The funds needed to develop a site were substantial, for capital went into acquiring mineral and timber rights, into the construction of a furnace and supplementary machinery, and usually into housing for the work force. The Hope furnace employed up to 75 men, with one-half of the workers normally engaged full time in gathering wood from nearby timber lands. Cordwood was converted into charcoal before entering the furnace in an extremely delicate and critical process. To serve as choppers, ore diggers, carters of wood and ore, molders, and firemen, the Browns had to recruit laborers with varying skills and to entice them with reasonably high wages. Finding men who were competent and sober was invariably a difficult task.

In addition to a sizable work force, the investors had to seek out capable supervisors to oversee day-to-day operations. The Hope partners hired one man, Rufus Hopkins, to serve in the capacity of general manager, with primary responsibilities in the areas of procuring timber, digging out ore, and handling the bookkeeping. The investors discovered it was more difficult to locate an accomplished founder who could supervise the technical aspects of the refining process. Because of limited knowledge about metallurgy, iron refining was as much an art as a science in the colonial era. A successful founder was usually an experienced man who had learned, largely through trial and error, how to combine charcoal and ore to produce iron with the desired characteristics. According to Paul Paskoff, the conversion of cordwood into charcoal was one of the most critical stages in the overall process because of the constant danger of fire, and because bad charcoal produced poor quality iron.

The Hope partners hired one founder who was unable to produce high-quality iron on a consistent basis, and he was replaced in 1768 by James Studefont, who had previously been employed at an iron plantation near Salisbury, Connecticut. From that date until Independence, the Hope furnace was a steady producer of pig iron. One experiment to cast high-quality pots and kettles at the Hope site was judged a failure. On another occasion, the partners considered a plan to operate a forge to complement the iron furnace. Some colonial forges merely removed the impurities from pig iron and thus refined it into what was commonly called bar iron, while others went one step further and actually fabricated bar iron into finished goods. In the end, however, the owners decided to restrict their operations largely to the production of basic pig iron.

The Browns marketed their iron through three distribution channels. Most of the pig iron was sent out on consignment to other mercantile firms in New York and England. A portion went to local merchants in Rhode Island, who were seeking a variety of salable commodities to include in cargoes destined for London and other foreign ports. Finally, the partners sold iron directly to owners of independent forges in the the New England area. In one complex business arrangement, the Browns sent pig iron to a forge in Massachusetts, received back refined bar iron in payment, and then hired several experienced workmen to transform the bar iron into finished nails.

Since it required a substantial initial investment and employed a fairly large number of workers, the colonial iron plantation had certain characteristics which singled it out as atypical for the period and made it a legitimate precursor of the nineteenth-century industrial plant. Because iron production was a continuous flow process, it demanded more labor discipline and regimentation than most colonial craftsmen were accustomed to in their occupational roles. The ironworks had a small managerial class as well, for merchant investors usually hired a general superintendent and a founder to oversee daily operations. Yet because it was tied to a charcoal technology, relied almost exclusively on waterpower, and was situated in a rural environment, the colonial iron industry still retained a premodern character.

Although the Browns had a broader range of activities and greater involvement in manufacturing than other businessmen, the family's pattern of business behavior was duplicated on a smaller scale by hundreds of all-purpose merchants throughout the colonies. The colonial businessman in the major ports was involved in a plethora of mercantile functions, from importing to exporting and from retailing to wholesaling, and he also occasionally diverted funds into the production of intermediate and finished goods for local and distant markets.

There was no distinct manufacturing class. With few exceptions, there were merely successful merchants who saw profit opportunities in diversifying their interests. For the most part, merchants personally managed their ancillary manufacturing enterprises. Iron production was, of course, an exception because of the large scale of enterprise and the technical knowledge required to operate a successful furnace.

The volume of business activity and the accumulation of mercantile wealth was greatest in the major port cities. Until the 1740s, Boston was the leading commercial center in North America, and its merchant families were the most prosperous on the continent. But Boston's commercial and population growth stagnated in the middle of the eighteenth century. The port lost much of its export trade in fish and its shipbuilding contracts to lesser rivals along the Massachusetts coast, such as Salem, Marblehead, and Gloucester. Meanwhile, Boston surrendered its preponderant position in the import trade with England after increased European demand for American wheat from the middle colonies led to more direct trade between the mother country and New York and Philadelphia in the 1750s.

By the late colonial period, Philadelphia had emerged as the most active port city. With over 30,000 residents, it was twice the size of Boston. On the basis of shipping tonnage cleared for overseas destinations, Philadelphia handled about 15 percent more foreign commerce than its older rival by 1770. The city had easy access to a heavily populated and highly productive agricultural hinterland in eastern Pennsylvania. The mercantile community first developed an active grain trade with the Caribbean and southern Europe and then build up connections with the mother country. Philadelphia became an entrepôt for finished goods, which were sent out to storekeepers in nearby towns and villages. The city's merchants were among the wealthiest on the continent; in the period from 1746 to 1775, Gary Nash found only three Boston merchants who left estates above £6,000 [$390,000], whereas Philadelphia had thirty-one in that category and several fortunes exceeded £15,000 [$975,000].

The third major port city in the northern colonies was New York. Like Boston, New York had been settled early in the seventeenth century, although by Dutchmen rather than Englishmen. After the British assumed control of the colony in 1664, the city's trade grew slowly but steadily. Until the mid-eighteenth century, New York was a more active port than Philadelphia. Sparked by expanding grain exports, New York merchants developed an active commerce with outlying farmers and storekeepers along the Hudson River and on Long Island. Yet the pace of population growth in the port's natural hinterland, while rapid in comparison with other regions, nonetheless failed to match the spectacular rate of increase in eastern Pennsylvania after 1750.

The most important commercial center in the south was Charleston, South Carolina. Its trading patterns and the organization of the mercantile community were distinctive. The strong demand for rice and indigo led to an extensive bilateral trade with the mother country. As a result, much of the port's trade was handled not by Charlestonians but rather by outside agents acting as representatives of mercantile firms based in London or Liverpool. The shipbuilding industry was also underdeveloped in comparison with northern ports, and most of Charleston's commerce was handled by English vessels. The city was therefore more a "shipping point" than a genuine "commercial center" or "general entrepôt," according to Jacob Price, and its mercantile community was more dependent on England for leadership. Indeed, the presence of so many British representatives explains in part why Charleston in 1770 shipped a larger volume of tonnage than New York with only half the urban population.

Two southern cities with an expanding mercantile community in the late colonial period were Norfolk, Virginia, and Baltimore, Maryland. With a population of around 6,500, Norfolk was the mainland's fifth largest city in 1774, while Baltimore ranked sixth with just under 6,000 residents. Despite their location—the Chesapeake area—neither city was involved extensively in the tobacco trade. In a recent survey of southern urbanization, Carville Earle and Ronald Hoffman discovered that these cities arose to serve primarily the requirements of the grain trade to the West Indies and southern Europe. Grain was a bulky, heavy, and perishable product. For the equivalent value of tobacco and grain, it took ten times more shipping tonnage and twenty to thirty more ships to handle the grain. Wheat generated more forward linkages in the marketing stage, and it supported a host of indigenous merchants. The rise of Norfolk and Baltimore and the growth of its mercantile community reflected the extent of diversification in Chesapeake agriculture in the late colonial period.

Individual merchants were among the wealthiest men in the society, and they played an important role in the political affairs of the colonies, especially in the north. In Massachusetts, for example, the merchant class dominated the upper chamber of the legislature after the 1690s; and by the mid-eighteenth century, it provided half of the leadership in the lower assembly. Merchants were similarly involved in the political life of the other northern colonies, and they had a minor role in southern governments.

This exercise of political power by the merchant class was another unique characteristic of the mainland colonies. Elsewhere around the world in the seventeenth and eighteenth centuries, large landowners were the social and economic elite and held a firm grasp on virtually all government offices. Even the accumulation of substantial wealth from mercantile activities would not buy respectability in most societies—not, for example, in France and Japan, two nations otherwise separated widely by geography, traditions, and culture. In England, merchants also ranked far below hereditary landowners, but upward mobility was not completely restricted. With sufficient wealth, a British merchant could acquire a country estate and later arrange to purchase a seat in Parliament.

In the mainland colonies, which had no domineering landholding class, merchants enjoyed high status from the outset. Moreover, they were not required to pass through the stage of becoming country gentlemen before exercising political power. Mobility was high too, for new mercantile wealth frequently emerged and forced a greater degree of turnover in leadership positions than elsewhere around the globe. The slow pace in business activity permitted merchants the leisure time to pursue vigorously political careers. They were normally respected and esteemed members of the community. This factor explains, in part, why outsiders have always perceived the United States as an excessively business-oriented society, highly attuned to mercantile values; indeed, no other society possesses such a long tradition of business leadership in its political system.

BIBLIOGRAPHICAL ESSAY

The two sources which I relied on most heavily for merchants were Stuart Bruchey, *The Colonial Merchant: Sources and Readings* (New

ARTISANS AND MERCHANTS 97

York: Harcourt, Brace & World, 1966) and the James Hedges, *The Browns of Providence Plantation: The Colonial Years* (Cambridge, Mass.: Harvard University Press, 1952). Valuable information on frontier merchants is found in Robert D. Mitchell, *Commericalism and Frontier: Perspectives on the Early Shenandoah Valley* (Charlottesville: University Press of Virginia, 1977). Three excellent articles on the port cities are Jacob Price, "Economic Functions and Growth of American Port Towns in the Eighteenth Century," in Donald Fleming and Bernard Bailyn, eds., *Perspectives in American History*, (Cambridge, Mass.: Harvard University Press, 1974), 8:123–88; Carville Earle and Ronald Hoffman, "Staple Crops and Urban Development in the Eighteenth-Century South," *ibid.* (1976), 10:7–77; and G. B. Warden, "The Distribution of Property in Boston, 1692–1775," *ibid.* 10:81–113. Gary Nash developed data on relative wealth in various ports in "Urban Wealth and Poverty in Pre-Revolutionary America," *Journal of Interdisciplinary History* (Spring 1976), pp. 545–84. His forthcoming book *The Urban Crucible* (Cambridge, Mass.: Harvard University Press) details further economic, social, and political issues in the major port cities. On the role of merchants in public life, see Robert Zemsky, *Merchants, Farmers, and River Gods: An Essay on Eighteenth-Century American Politics* (Boston: Gambit Press, 1971). Paul Paskoff is currently revising for publication his dissertation, "Colonial Merchant-Manufacturers and Iron, A Study in Capital Transformation, 1725–1775" (Ph.D. dissertation, Johns Hopkins University, 1976).

For information on artisans, a good starting point is Carl Bridenbaugh, *The Colonial Craftsman* (New York: New York University Press, 1950). Also valuable are Richard Morris, *Government and Labor in Early America* (New York: Columbia University Press, 1946) and Blanche Hazard, *Organization of the Boot and Shoe Industry in Massachusetts before 1875* (Cambridge, Mass.: Harvard University Press, 1921). Newer studies are Joseph A. Goldenberg, *Shipbuilding in Colonial America* (Charlottesville: University Press of Virginia, 1976); Stephanie Wolfe, *Urban Village: Population, Community, and Family Structure in Germantown, Pennsylvania, 1683–*

1800 (Princeton, N.J.: Princeton University Press, 1976); and Wolfe, "Artisans and the Occupational Structure of an Industrial Town: 18th-Century Germantown, Pa.," in Glenn Porter and William Mulligan, eds., *Social Change in Early Industrial Communities,* Working Papers from the Regional Economic History Research Center (Greenville, Delaware, 1977), pp. 33–56. Some good data on rural artisans is found in James Lemon, *The Best Poor Man's Country* (Baltimore, Md.: Johns Hopkins University Press, 1972). The locations of iron furnaces and forges plus the geographic distribution of silversmiths are in Lester Cappon, ed., *Atlas of Early American History* (Princeton, N.J.: Princeton University Press, 1976).

On the political activities of artisans in the 1760s and 1770s, see Charles Olton, *Artisans for Independence* (Syracuse, N.Y.: Syracuse University Press, 1975); Eric Foner, *Tom Paine and Revolutionary America* (New York: Oxford University Press, 1976); and the essays by Gary Nash, Eric Foner, and Dirk Hoerder in the Alfred F. Young, ed., *The American Revolution: Explorations in the History of American Radicalism* (DeKalb: Northern Illinois University Press, 1976).

Section Two

MONEY AND TAXES

FROM the vantage point of the twentieth century, the colonial monetary system was institutionally undeveloped. Absent entirely were specialized financial institutions such as commercial banks and organized capital markets. Demand deposits, savings accounts, bank loans, and government bond issues were unknown in the colonies. The money supply was composed largely of gold and silver coins which circulated freely throughout the economy.

Financial services were provided in limited fashion first by merchants who granted book credit on the sale of merchandise and who, along with planters, occasionally were sources of direct monetary loans. In addition, colonial legislatures augmented the money supply with paper currency issues and sometimes loaned moderate sums to a broad spectrum of their citizens with land to offer as collateral. Yet despite its shortcomings by modern standards, the monetary system functioned sufficiently well to support a rapidly growing agricultural-commercial economy with very high income levels. This was true in part because the colonies were able to make use, indirectly, of the financial services available in London, where money markets were far more institutionally advanced.

The mainland colonies were unique by contemporary standards because of an extremely low overall tax burden and the innovative use of government-issue paper money. Moreover, a link existed between these two characteristics; it was the lack of adequate tax revenues to finance a series of military campaigns against the French, Spanish, and various native American tribes on the frontier that initially led colonial legislatures to experiment with the creation of paper currency to meet immediate wartime expenses. The colonists had looked to Parliament for reimbursement for the costs of defending and expanding the British empire, and it had generally accepted the financial burden.

Over the last two decades of the colonial era, however, the king's ministers adopted new policies designed to shift more of the tax burden for defending North America and the Atlantic shipping lanes to the colonists themselves and to restrict, and perhaps even outlaw, the use of paper money. These two issues of contention—paper money and especially new taxes—were in the forefront of the political and economic dispute between England and her colonies just prior to the movement for independence.

CHAPTER VI

MONEY AND POLITICS

I RRESPECTIVE of the controversy over paper currency, the major component of the colonial money stock was specie. In part because Parliament did not allow the export of English coin from the British Isles, and because it refused to grant permission for the establishment of a separate mint overseas (except for a brief experiment in Massachusetts in the 1650s), the colonies relied primarily on silver and gold coins from Spain's New World mines for everyday monetary transactions and a store of value. To assist her colonies in attracting and retaining foreign specie, the mother country, in 1705, permitted them to overvalue by one-third foreign coins relative to English money in domestic transactions. The official exchange rate for "lawful money" on the mainland thus became 133 colonial "pounds" for every 100 English pounds, although market rates often fluctuated above and below this par figure.

Even with the overvaluation of foreign coins, the colonists complained almost constantly about a dearth of specie. Although sales of foodstuffs to the Caribbean and southern Europe produced a steady inflow of gold and silver coins, contemporaries cited the persistent trade deficits with England and claimed that purchases of British imports caused an excessive drain of specie to the mother country. Commonplace in the seventeenth and eighteenth centuries were merchants' grumblings about the stagnation of colonial commerce, coupled with predictions of hard times, all because of allegedly insufficient quantities of hard money in circulation.

It is difficult to accept the colonists' complaints at face value, however. There is no firm evidence suggesting that the colonies were plagued by a severe shortage of specie. Merchants and farmers in England were voicing similar complaints about the alleged inadequacy of the monetary stock during this period. Yet according to colonial rhetoric, it was to England that specie was constantly being "drained."

Aggregate data on price levels point toward another conclusion about the adequacy of the money stock. In the eighteenth century, prices in the colonies rose steadily. The prices of twenty commodities in Pennsylvania rose by 24 percent in silver from 1720 to 1774; in Boston the silver price of wheat was up 62 percent over the same period. Since we have no evidence of a change in the velocity of money, the price data suggest that the money stock was growing at a faster pace than the produciton of goods and services. Had world specie supplies been genuinely short, then prices over this era would have undoubtedly fallen—a phenomenon which the U.S. economy actually experienced during the deflationary years from 1866 to 1896, when the stock of money expanded at a slower pace than goods and services. During the colonial period, the outpouring of specie from Latin American mines was rapidly distributed throughout the Atlantic economies, including the mainland English colonies. The supply of specie was not deficient.

Another factor often overlooked in discussions of the size of specie stocks in a given economy is the domestic demand for money. As Dennis Flynn has recently argued in an analysis of sixteenth-century Spain, the composition of that nation's monetary stock was a reflection not only of the supply of specie available but also of the aggregate demand for it. Despite a century-long influx of specie from Latin America, Spain contained virtually no gold or silver coins at the end of the sixteenth century. To serve as a medium of domestic exchange, the Spanish government introduced copper coins into the monetary system, and the volume was large enough to accommodate the domestic demand for money. Specie went abroad to acquire foreign goods and services. The Spanish population required just so much money to accommodate their level of domestic economic activity, and this aggregate demand was met mostly by copper coins. The excess money in the financial system, namely specie, was spent in the international market.

In the thirteen English colonies, the size of the specie stock was likewise influenced by local demand. If the colonists had genuinely wished to increase the availability of gold and silver coins over the long run, they had the option of reducing the volume of imports and of foregoing entirely the use of domestic money substitutes such as paper currency and commodity money. In short, the role of gold and silver in the colonial money stock was influenced as much by demand forces as by supply. Overall, the colonists held about as much gold and silver as they demanded.

To be sure, specie shortages of sufficient magnitude to dampen trade were periodically experienced in the colonies, but the condition was temporary rather than chronic. Shifting prices for sterling bills of exchange—in other words, foreign exchange rates—kept the monetary system in long-run equilibium. The mechanism functioned briefly as follows: from the sales of goods overseas, colonial exporters generated inflows of sterling, which they, in turn, sold to local importers of English goods with debts payable in London. Although foreign exchange markets were likewise institutionally immature, this system operated relatively smoothly so long as imports and exports were in balance. During certain years, however, and especially late in the era, imports ran consistently ahead of exports. When the trade imbalance persisted, the colonies were faced with an accumulation of debts and a growing balance of payments deficit vis-à-vis the mother country.

Normally, these payments deficits were financed through the voluntary extension of liberal credit terms to colonial buyers by English merchants. In London, unlike the colonies, large amounts of capital were readily available at modest interest rates, and merchants drew upon those funds to finance their overseas sales. At times, however, colonial debts temporarily exceeded the ability or the willingness of the English merchants to carry them. The subsequent efforts of colonial debtors to cover, almost simultaneously, their deficit accounts drove up the price of foreign exchange so high that many found it less costly to forego the acquisition of sterling bills completely and remit instead specie to England. When this chain of events affected the inhabitants of a given colony, its specie stock was sharply reduced, and its domestic trade was hampered somewhat by the financial dislocation.

Fortunately, these monetary disturbances were self-correcting. The high sterling rates raised the effective prices of all British goods and led to a curtailment in a colony's imports. The reduced purchases of

British merchandise translated into a lowered demand for sterling in the ensuing months, and the exchange rate correspondingly fell. Specie exports to England would automatically cease. Meanwhile, trade surpluses with the Caribbean and southern Europe continued to produce a regular inflow of gold and silver coins, and the colony's money stock was eventually replenished.

In sum, the colonies were full participants in an emerging international financial system, with gold and silver at its base. Since the flow of specie from nation to nation and to their colonies was not unduly restricted, the distribution of the total money stock was never heavily skewed in favor of one region or to the disadvantage of another. Cycles of specie contraction followed by replenishment were frequent in the colonies and elsewhere. Fundamental market forces were at work in the form of relative prices for internationally traded products and fluctuations in foreign exchange rates. They were identified by Adam Smith as the "invisible hands," which kept the Western world's monetary and economic systems in general equilibrium.

In addition to the use of coin, the colonists found other means of expediting domestic transactions. Wampum, the polished shells valued by native Americans, was accepted as lawful money for a short time in the seventeenth century. The ageless system of direct barter was exceedingly common, especially in frontier areas remote from active markets. Within the mercantile community, the extension of book credit in anticipation of the receipt of a return shipment of similarly valued goods was a regular practice. Merchants, large and small, at home and abroad, exchanged goods with other merchants and local consumers through the convenient medium of bookkeeping entries.

Although modern economic analysis excludes book credit in the measurement of the money supply, several scholars of colonial finance believe that twentieth-century monetary theories may be too narrow for an understanding of eighteenth-century finance. Joseph Ernst in his influential study of money and politics from 1755 to 1775 concluded that the inclusion of book credit in the definition of the colonial money supply was extremely beneficial in explaining movements in foreign exchange rates. In subsequent research, Robert Craig West has also called for more serious consideration of book credit in the financial system. He hypothesized that book credit may have played a role analogous to demand deposits in the modern economy. In the more advanced commercial areas, Ernst and West suggest that it served as the most common medium of domestic exchange. The validity of this approach remains unproven, however, and the measurement of the extent of book credit and its impact on the colonial economy awaits further research.

In some colonies, valuable commodities resistant to spoilage were designated as legal tender in the payment of debts and the fulfillment of contracts. Tobacco provides the best example. In Virginia and Maryland, this form of commodity money was an important component of the monetary system. Taxes, duties, court fees, and the salaries of clergymen were normally payable in tobacco. To expedite even further this medium of exchange, Virginia established official storehouses where the depositors of tobacco received warehouse receipts which then circulated conveniently as money. The main drawbacks of commodity money were that it fluctuated in value, moving in unison with the market price of tobacco, and its volume was limited to the amount of tobacco in local warehouses.

PAPER MONEY

The colonial legislatures also experimented with the issuance of paper currency. The paper money only supplemented specie, which remained the main component of the money stock, and never actually superseded it in terms of purchasing power. By 1755, after the Virginia assembly had finally acted, every colony had emitted some variant of paper money. Roger Weiss has argued that only for limited periods in Pennsylvania, New York, and perhaps in Virginia during the 1760s did paper currency ever approach 50 percent of a colony's total money stock. In the New England colonies the *nominal* or face value of currency issues was often quite high, but because of depreciation, paper normally represented less than 5 percent of the purchasing power of the specie coins in circulation.

The North American colonies were among the earliest political units in modern history to test the viability of paper currency as a medium of exchange and to persist in its use. The Chinese had preceded the colonies in issuing sizable volumes of paper notes, but they had abandoned the practice in the fifteenth century. No European state had previously authorized the issuance of paper money on a vast scale. In the mother country, the Bank of England and the government Treasury issued notes and Exchequer bills in the eighteenth century, but these instruments never became legal tender in the payment of private debts. The high denominations of these notes and bills, a £20 minimum for the Bank of England and a £100 minimum for the Treasury after 1709, effectively prevented them from circulating widely and becoming an everyday medium of exchange.

Most economic and political leaders in England strongly favored an exclusively specie system. They viewed paper currency as at best a novel aberration. For some, it was a matter of deep-seated principle: paper money violated a presumed economic axiom; it was inherently unsound and probably corrupt. Since it had no underlying base, paper therefore was likely to depreciate in value and disrupt, if not destroy, any economy. Most of the king's ministers associated with the administration of colonial affairs were prejudiced in varying degrees against paper money, although they frequently condoned its issuance as a temporary expedient.

In the colonies, on the other hand, paper currency was widely supported as a legitimate feature of the financial system. The focus of the colonial leadership was more on practicalities than abstract monetary principles. The relative degree of consensus was surprising, given the very controversial course of American monetary history in the nineteenth century. During the colonial years, however, few irreconcilable arguments broke out between hard money diehards and paper-money advocates, as occurred so frequently and vociferously during the later Jacksonian and Reconstruction eras. Indeed the colonial paper-money issue defies easy class analysis, as Leslie Brock argued in a penetrating dissertation written in 1941 and now only recently published. Although paper normally depreciated to the detriment of creditors, it was enthusiastically endorsed by many members of the elite economic classes who dominated colonial legislatures and who were more often creditors than debtors in domestic transactions.

The initial emission of paper currency came in Massachusetts in 1690, and the circumstances of its issuance set a pattern that was repeated in colony after colony. An underfinanced military campaign against French Quebec failed, and the returning soldiers who had not been paid the promised wages were on the verge of mutiny. The colony's treasury was almost empty, and with no banks or other private sources of loanable funds, the Massachusetts legislature fell upon the expediency of issuing £7,000 ($445,000) in paper bills of credit. In an effort to uphold the value of the bills, they were made legal tender in the payment of provincial taxes, and after 1691 at a 5 percent advance over the face amount. Upon their receipt at the Treasury, the bills were to be promptly destroyed. Thus, this deviation from established financial practice was designed to be temporary and self-liquidating. In this first instance, the paper bills were retired in due course, and the monetary experiment was deemed a huge success.

In later years in Massachusetts and elsewhere, new emergencies continually arose, and colonial legislatures resorted to the printing and issuing of paper money to finance government expenditures. Usually a financial crisis had military origins, and the imperial officials in London reluctantly approved (invariably after the fact) fresh emissions of paper.

Since this system of currency finance functioned so effectively from the colonists' standpoint, legislatures discovered other reasons for authorizing new emissions. In some cases, especially Pennsylvania in the 1720s, the justification was the stimulation of lethargic trade; in other cases—for example, Maryland in 1733—the explanation was merely the convenience of the inhabitants because of an alleged shortage of specie and commodity money for daily transactions. As time passed, the expiration dates of the individual issues lengthened from just two or three years to ten or more years; old bills received in tax payments were not always burned but were occasionally reissued; and a colony's various emissions began to overlap one another in time. When a colony's paper depreciated heavily, as happened in New England and South Carolina during the first half of the eighteenth century, the legislature often authorized an exchange of "new" tenor bills for the outstanding "old" tenor bills at some fixed ratio. In short, the perpetuation of a long series of temporary emissions gave many colonies de facto a permanent system of paper currency to augment the local supply of specie and commodity money.

The terms of currency issues differed in all thirteen colonies, which makes generalization difficult. Variations existed in the security or backing for the bills, the length of issue, the method of retirement, interest-rate features, and legal-tender provisions. For our purposes, the issues can be placed in two broad categories, with the source of funds for retirement—whether public tax revenues or loan repayments by private citizens—the distinguishing characteristic. In some colonies both types were outstanding at the same time.

Given the universally modest level of taxation and the correspondingly small accumulation of specie in almost every colony's treasury, legislatures frequently authorized the emission of paper currency to pay pressing military expenses and other outstanding government debts. The economic consequences were twofold. This action meant that those who accepted the paper bills in payment had actually been forced to make involuntary loans to the colonial government. Simultaneously, it postponed until the assigned retirement date of the bills the collection of taxes for ongoing expenses, which explains in large part why such legislative acts were popular, since, given the option, most individuals—then and now—preferred to delay taxes rather than pay them currently.

In some instances, the paper bills carried no interest rate, and thus became a "free" loan for the colonial government. (The greenback dollars issued during the Civil War and surprisingly still in limited circulation today are another example of an interest-free loan forced upon holders by government.) On other occasions, even within the same colony, the terms of issue provided for the acceptance of the bills in the payment of future taxes at some stated premium, often 5 percent. In yet another variation, the interest associated with a given issue of currency compounded during the years it remained outstanding.

In addition to the fairness of compensating noteholders for accepting paper in lieu of specie, the interest-rate feature served to hold up the value of the currency and diminish or even prevent its depreciation. The only drawback was that many individuals began to view the bills as investments rather than everyday money when the retirement date approached. When citizens hoarded interest-bearing paper currency for its investment qualities, they prevented its wide circulation and denied the colony the convenience of an expanded money supply.

Not every issue was the result of a financial crisis or emergency; some legislatures simply voted to increase the local money supply in the hope of stimulating domestic trade and attracting more foreign commerce. Richard Lester has written extensively about new currency issues in Pennsylvania in 1723 and 1729 that were intended to boost economic activity and overcome mild recessions. According to Lester, the emissions were very successful, and the legislature largely achieved its goals.

Convinced of the beneficial effects of an increased money supply in New York and Pennsylvania, the Maryland legislature, in 1733, decided to test the usefulness of paper as a medium of exchange. Much of the Pennsylvania paper had already spilled over the Maryland border and was readily accepted in provincial trade. The Maryland currency was distributed throughout the colony on a per capita basis to all persons subject to taxation. Every taxable individual was given 30 shillings ($98), with the amounts allocated for indentured servants and slaves turned over to the master.

In all the cases cited above, the legislatures relied solely on provincial tax revenues to provide sufficient funds to retire the currency issues. As a rule, special taxes were imposed for this purpose. Two common sources of revenue were property taxes and head taxes; in the Chesapeake colonies an export tax on tobacco shipments went toward retiring the outstanding paper. In most cases outside of New England, the taxes were collected gradually over the life of the issue and accumulated in a sinking fund. Maryland, for example, built up a substantial reserve from export taxes on tobacco; the colony's tax revenues were transmitted to London and invested in the stock of the Bank of England. As a result, the colony had the soundest currency system on the mainland. In other instances, the taxes were imposed only in the last year or two before the scheduled retirement. The impending implementation of plans to collect these special taxes led many legislatures to consider favorably alternative proposals to reissue the old currency or replace it with a fresh emission of paper bills.

In a second broad category of currency issues, colonial legislatures established loan offices which loaned funds to resident property holders with land and improvements as security. Commonly called land banks in the eighteenth century, that term would be institutionally inappropriate today because these government offices accepted no deposits and negotiated only real estate loans. Every colony except Virginia created loan offices in the eighteenth century.

To guarantee a fairly wide distribution of the paper money, limits were usually placed on the sums available to individuals. In 1737, for example, the New York legislature authorized loans of from £25 ($1,625) to £100 ($6,500) at 5 percent interest for twelve years against mortgages on properties valued at twice the amount of the loan. In this primarily agricultural economy, land was the safest security for most financial obligations, and the only asset widely held by the white residents. Under these loan arrangements, there was no drain on the public coffers, since the original borrowers, not the taxpayers, were individually responsible for repaying their loans and ultimately retiring the note issue.

This lending mechanism for the issuance of paper bills was advantageous in several respects. The colony's circulating medium was enlarged, which pleased most citizens because the negotiation of small transactions became much easier. The loans also provided a source of investment funds for a colonial economy chronically short of capital, and at interest rates, typically 5 to 6 percent, which were far below the going rates for the limited funds available in the private sector from wealthy merchants and planters. In this respect, the government loan offices performed a legitimate and important banking function.

Meanwhile, the interest revenue accruing to the colony's treasury contributed significantly to the cost of maintaining government services. The burden on taxpayers was correspondingly lightened. In Massachusetts in the 1720s, the towns administered the currency loans and kept the interest revenue for their own benefit. In Pennsylvania and New York, E. James Ferguson has shown that interest revenues alone were sometimes sufficient to cover all of a colony's nonmilitary expenses—a figure often no higher than £5,000 ($325,000) per year.

In terms of the colonies' relationship with the mother country, the most controversial features of all the paper-money emissions were the legal-tender provisions. In an effort to generate a steady demand for the paper bills, most colonies made them legal tender in the payment of public fees and taxes to the treasury, and at government loan offices where appropriate. The acceptance of the bills at full face value in all public transactions was normally the principal factor supporting the market value of the paper relative to specie and foreign exchange.

Over the years, pressure mounted in some colonies to make paper currency legal tender in private transactions as well. Many legislators felt that this added feature aided in maintaining the value of the currency and simultaneously encouraged economic activity generally. At times, legislatures asserted that such provisions were absolutely essential, and they incorporated them in acts authorizing fresh emissions.

Difficulties arose, however, when debtors attempted to pay off old obligations with paper that had depreciated during the intervening months or years. In these situations, creditors often demanded specie or expressed a willingness to accept paper money only at its current market value. Many disputes over the proper settlement of old debts in colonies with heavily depreciated paper eventually ended up in the colonial courts for adjudication.

One group deeply concerned about the danger of court-ordered debt settlements in depreciated currency were British merchants with extensive sales on account. The merchants feared that anticipated profits on transactions in goods would be reduced and might even be converted into losses if they were forced to accept in payment money worth considerably less, in relation to specie and British sterling, than it had been worth on the original sales date. This group felt exceedingly vulnerable to potential abuse in the colonial courts, which were thousands of miles across the ocean.

Based largely in London, these merchants were in a favorable position to exert varying degrees of political influence over British colonial policy. In negotiations with the Board of Trade and Parliamentary ministers, London merchants first tried to seek the disallowance of all colonial acts with provisions that made paper currency lawful money in private transactions. But faced with the intransigence of some legislatures and the generally casual attitude of crown officials toward colonial affairs prior to the 1760s, the English merchants later accelerated their demands and asked increasingly for a complete ban on all legal tender provisions, public as well as private. In some colonies where depreciation was viewed as a constant threat, they advocated the elimination of paper currency altogether.

Responding to the direct pressure from English merchants, while at the same time moving toward a general plan for greater administrative control over the mainland colonies, Parliament passed two separate acts, in 1751 and 1764, relating to paper money. The first act was aimed solely at the New England colonies, where, in addition to South Carolina, depreciation had been heaviest. It restricted the life of new emissions in Rhode Island, Connecticut, Massachusetts, and New Hampshire to just two years, and it prohibited the designation of the bills as legal tender in all private transactions.

The path for this legislation had been cleared somewhat in 1747, when Parliament voted to reimburse the four New England colonies for their expenses in connection with the military campaign against Louisburg, in French Canada, in 1745. Massachusetts had used its £183,649 share ($11.7 million) to retire all the outstanding paper in circulation and thereby return to a primarily specie standard. The Act of 1751 was not therefore especially punitive. Moreover, during the next quarter century, the four northern colonies used all the leeway in the law to issue substantial amounts of the permissible two-year paper, which was not lawful money in private matters. For the most part, however, specie was the major component of the real money stock in New England after midcentury, and the controversy over paper currency shifted south.

During the Parliamentary debate in 1751, the possibility of extending the act to all the mainland colonies was raised, but a split in the ranks of London merchants temporarily diverted that movement. The depreciation rates of currencies emitted in Pennsylvania, New York, New Jersey, Delaware, and Maryland were modest in comparison to the record established in New England in the 1740s. The agents representing these colonies' interests argued for an exemption from the act, and they gained momentarily the support of merchants trading heavily in those provinces. Except in South Carolina, which had been singled out earlier and denied permission to declare any new emissions legal tender in private debts after 1731, English merchants had not been exposed to excessive currency risks outside of New England, and they were willing to follow a wait-and-see policy toward the other colonies.

By the early 1760s, however, attitudes in England had altered. Virginia, the colony with the largest bilateral trade with Britain, had issued its first paper money in 1755, with full legal-tender provisions. Consequently, an increased number of London merchants faced greater exposure to currency risks. More complaints arose about the alleged inequities of settlements in colonial courts, and especially in comparison to the situation in New England, where all private debts were strictly on a specie basis. Although specific instances of actual losses were few, except perhaps in North Carolina, the vacillating

London merchants had concluded by 1764 that, on balance, the extension of the restriction on legal-tender provisions to all the mainland
colonies was in their best interest.

Meanwhile, the crown and Parliament had developed more interest
in exerting control over colonial affairs generally. Under consideration
inside the ministry headed by George Grenville was a proposal to
create a comprehensive currency system for all the mainland colonies
under the supervision of the mother country; the paper was to be
secured by a special fund generated from the revenues of a proposed
stamp tax. But a strong bias against all forms of paper money
prevailed in the Grenville ministry. Finally the currency legislation
and the tax proposals were separated.

The Currency Act of 1764 applied only to the colonies outside of
New England. The law expanded the previous ban on legal-tender
provisions to include not only private debts but inexplicably public obligations as well, at least as interpreted by the Board of Trade.
Whereas the four northernmost provinces had adjusted readily to the
earlier act, the remaining colonies were in a more combative mood by
1764, and they resisted. Colonies like New York and Pennsylvania,
which had managed paper-money systems for decades with only
gradual depreciation, felt the new regulations were unjustified and un-
reasonable. In those two colonies, paper money actually comprised
from one-third to one-half of the real money stock.

In defiance, some legislatures continued to authorize new paper
emissions with legal-tender features and then coerced their governors
into submitting the laws to British officials for approval. In some
instances, colonial acts were summarily disallowed, but in other cases
irregularities were overlooked. The British officials rejected, for
example, two South Carolina acts in 1770 and 1772 and one from
New York in 1769 because of unacceptable legal-tender clauses. Yet,
crown ministers in 1770 let stand a Pennsylvania act which made the
new bills legal tender at the colony's loan office.

After 1764, the colonies sought revisions in the rules pertaining to
the lawfulness of paper currency in meeting public obligations. In

1770, New York's agents and their London allies lobbied hard for a special act giving the colony permission to make its paper legal tender for all public purposes, and Parliament granted New York an exemption from the 1764 law. Other colonies asked for similar consideration. Finally, in 1773, Parliament revised the law and permitted the colonies to declare their currency issues legal tender in all public payments. The ban on paper-money settlements of private debts remained in force. There the matter rested until the outbreak of the war.

After decades of wrangling, the question was largely resolved to the general satisfaction of the colonies and the overseas merchants. The British merchants got protection from the risk of losses stemming from the depreciation of colonial paper, and the legislatures retained the authority to emit new currency in anticipation of taxes and through provincial loan offices.

Why this currency matter proved so difficult to reconcile has perplexed historians. Recently Joseph Ernst has pointed to a link between the shifting views of the English merchant class and the level of foreign exchange rates for sterling bills. The vacillations of British officials reflected, Ernst argues, the vacillating outlook of London merchants. When a colony's debts were weighty and the sterling exchange rate rose way above par, the merchants became especially fearful that colonial courts might settle old debts in depreciated paper. If a currency act came before the Board of Trade while sterling rates in that colony were high, the merchants were almost certain to oppose it. On the other hand, when sales in a given colony were slack and sterling rates were near par or lower, the same merchants were likely to revise their position and favor the emission of new paper because they hoped it might stimulate commerce and increase their lagging exports. In sum, Ernst suggests that fluctuations in British attitudes about the merits of paper money can be explained in large part by fluctuations in colonial indebtedness and sterling rates.

The British merchant class was not the only group to damn the consequences of currency depreciation; a century later most professional economists and historians viewed colonial monetary practices even more harshly. By the late-nineteenth and early-twentieth centuries, depreciation was condemned as representing not merely a case of irresponsible economics but moral corruption as well. As happens so often, these scholars had their eye focused almost exclusively on current issues, and looking for "lessons" from the past, they foisted their hard money biases on their defenseless forebears. Beginning with the pioneering studies of Richard Lester in the 1930s, and E. James Ferguson in the early 1950s, however, the older doctrinaire outlook has undergone steady modification. The modern judgment is more benign and tolerant, even positive in certain respects.

Paper money was neither as harmful as its critics alleged nor as essential as its proponents asserted. There is no reason to believe that its existence or absence had any more than the slightest impact on income levels in the colonies. Paper currency was merely one feature of the financial system, and in many colonies it comprised only a fraction of the real money stock. Indeed, Roger Weiss has shown that an inverse relationship normally existed between the nominal amount of currency in circulation and its contribution in terms of purchasing power to a colony's money stock. Virginia is an example of a colony that prospered and maintained a viable financial system without paper currency until the first emission in 1755. The New England colonies were largely on a specie standard after midcentury. Thus, the argument advanced by many colonial legislatures in their negotiations with the mother country after 1760, that paper currency was essential for their economic survival, must be discounted heavily. The underlying issue here was political control not economics.

On the other hand, the contention of the colonial legislators that paper currency was convenient and useful and produced few ill effects had considerable merit. Since no colony established a fixed exchange ratio between its currency and specie or sterling, Gresham's law—that good money (specie) drives out bad (paper)—never became fully operational.* Currency maintained a market value relative to specie, and ir-

---

* The only fixed ratio was a limit on the overvaluation of foreign coin vis-à-vis sterling; the ratio was £133 in foreign coin to £100 sterling.

respective of its level of depreciation, paper remained in circulation and fulfilled in varying degrees its function as a medium of exchange. Moreover, its drop in value was rarely precipitous but extended over months or years. Those colonists who anticipated a decline in the value of currency often used a two-tier pricing system for tangible goods to compensate for the probable slippage in the market rate for paper. They quoted higher prices for goods sold for paper money rather than for specie, just as retailers today offer discounts to customers who pay in cash rather than with credit cards.

In the colonial era, few individuals held large paper balances or lived on fixed incomes. Bank deposits did not exist. Depreciation was thus less of a threat than today in terms of destroying accumulated wealth or eroding real incomes. Colonists seeking a monetary store of wealth invariably held specie. To the extent that wealth was eroded somewhat by depreciation, urban residents, who were more deeply involved in money transactions, probably felt the effects more than farmers.

The depreciation of currencies can also be viewed as an alternate method of taxation. Legislatures frequently issued new paper in financial emergencies to avoid a sharp hike in current taxes. To the extent that the currency depreciated and was never fully redeemed, the real tax burden fell on all those who held the paper over the years. In many ways, this became a relatively painless system of taxation, for the incidence was spread out over a long period of time. The recipient of paper merely lost a few percentage points in the value of the money when the next transaction occurred. The net effect was analogous to a modern sales tax. In this case, it is not clear whether the losses from currency depreciation fell mainly on merchants or on their customers.

When sales were made on credit, however, merchants became more vulnerable the longer an account remained unpaid. In the domestic trade, merchants found profit margins sufficiently high to cover small monetary losses on debt settlements, which became simply another cost of doing business. Only English merchants, who had debts strung out for long periods of time across an ocean, wanted ironclad protection against currency risks. In truth, colonial courts generally sought equity in their proceedings and usually took into account the changing market value of paper currency in settling debts. English creditors may have fared somewhat worse than local creditors in colonial courtrooms, but the London merchants' fears of grossly unfair treatment were based on isolated cases and were much overdrawn.

Until recently, scholars had assumed a close link between the volume of paper currency in circulation and the rate of inflation experienced in the colonies over the eighteenth century. A comparison of prices for basic commodities in Philadelphia, Boston, and England shows clearly that inflation proceeded at a faster pace in the colonies than in the mother country. Yet when Robert Craig West ran a series of regressions to measure the correlation between the issuance of paper money and the rate of inflation in Boston, Philadelphia, New York, and Charleston from 1700 to 1764, his results were largely negative. Only in Boston during the period from 1720 to 1749, when the volume of paper in circulation was extremely high, was there any significant statistical correlation. In Philadelphia, where we have the most reliable data on prices and paper money, the statistical analysis revealed no meaningful relationship. With the exception of Boston, West concluded that there was no proof that the volume of paper currency in circulation caused colonial sterling prices to escalate at a faster rate than English sterling prices.

In many colonies the mechanism of distributing new currency was probably of greater significance than the volume of paper issued. The government loan offices provided funds, through the issuance of currency, to a large number of farmers at very moderate interest rates, usually 6 percent or lower. Alternative sources of loanable funds, in the absence of private financial institutions, were unavailable at comparable interest rates. For an economy almost as short of capital as it was of labor, these mortgage loans permitted the colonists to expand more rapidly the productive base of their economy, and thus the loans encouraged economic development.

The denominational structure of paper-currency issues was also designed to make monetary transactions more convenient for the general public. Specie coins were generally high-value money. In a study of the Philadelphia money market in the 1740s, John Hanson discovered that the lowest denomination coin in general circulation was valued at 7½ shillings, which represented about three days in wages for an unskilled labor and is the equivalent of approximately $25 in 1980 prices. Colonial paper, in contrast, was issued in much smaller denominations. Four colonies issued currency in sums as low as one shilling ($3.25). Hanson reviewed the denominational structure of the currency in Pennsylvania, New York, Maryland, Rhode Island, New Jersey, and Virginia, and he found that the volume of bills issued in amounts under 5 shillings ($16) ranged from a low of 40 percent in New York to a high of 81 percent in Rhode Island. Because of the increased number of small notes in circulation, transaction costs were almost certainly lower in the colonies than in the mother country, and this factor may have contributed to the growth in per capita incomes.

Finally, there remains the proposition that paper money was an important factor in overcoming economic slowdowns in some colonies. The fresh emission of paper created an immediate surge in demand for goods, and, according to this hypothesis, the revival of commerce was normally sustained. Based on his detailed examination of Pennsylvania in the 1720s, Richard Lester advanced this argument in the 1930s. In this instance the sample size has unfortunately remained too small to determine whether the issue of fresh paper was a major cause of colonial economic recoveries or whether it merely coincided with them. Nonetheless, the issuance of paper currency and the sudden increase in the size of the money stock in Pennsylvania and elsewhere clearly failed to retard economic recoveries, and in certain years probably contributed somewhat to increased economic activity. Over the entire colonial era, however, it remains doubtful whether paper currency had much influence on the overall level of output or on per capita incomes.

During the last twenty-five years of colonial status, the paper money controversy was responsible for much of the turmoil in Anglo-American relations. By the 1760s, more than just economics was at stake; compromise solutions were readily available but neither side was in a mood to give them serious consideration.

Unlike their strategies in developing the earlier navigation acts, the British never developed a comprehensive plan for a colonial monetary system. The use of currency evolved piecemeal on a colony-by-colony basis, with provincial legislatures providing the initiative. The record of the Board of Trade and Parliamentary ministers in approving or disallowing colonial monetary acts was contradictory and discriminatory; their rulings depended on the personalities holding office at home and abroad, the efforts of colonial agents in London, the previous financial performance of the colonies in question, and the prevailing attitude of the wavering London merchants. The Currency Act of 1764 was poorly drafted, for it implied that colonial paper could no longer become legal tender in public as well as private transactions. Thereafter, in discussions about possible revisions, British officials failed to heed the advice of Benjamin Franklin, who recommended that simply a ban on legal-tender status for paper in all foreign debts would resolve the one point of contention between the legislatures and the London merchants.

By the same token, the argument of some colonial legislatures that legal-tender status for paper in all private transactions was an absolutely essential feature of any currency act cannot be accepted as valid. In numerous instances, and in New England by statute after 1751, colonies found it advantageous to issue paper which was lawful money only in public transactions. Except in Maryland, where a reserve fund of sterling and Bank of England stock provided security, the main support for the value of currency was the steady public demand to discharge taxes or repay mortgage loans. No positive correlation exists between the inclusion of private legal-tender provisions and the maintenance of par values for colonial currencies. Vastly more important was the colonial legislatures' resolve to vote the taxes required to retire the outstanding paper and the persistence of the loan offices in collecting mortgage debts.

In 1773, when Parliament finally agreed to permit the emission of legal-tender currency for public debts in every mainland colony, the issue was largely settled. It was not a major grievance on the eve of independence. The one unresolved economic question was instead the colonial contribution to the tax revenues of the British empire.

BIBLIOGRAPHICAL ESSAY

Three important books on colonial finance are Curtis Nettels, *Money Supply of the American Colonies before 1720* (Madison: University of Wisconsin Press, 1934); Leslie Brock's published 1941 dissertation, *The Currency System of the American Colonies 1700–1764* (New York: Arno Press, 1975); and Joseph Ernst, *Money and Politics in America, 1755–1775* (Chapel Hill: University of North Carolina Press, 1973).

A contemporary analysis of the currency issue was Benjamin Franklin's "Remarks and Facts Relative to the American Paper Money," written in 1767, and published in Benjamin Labaree, ed., *The Papers of Benjamin Franklin* (New Haven: Yale University Press, 1970), 14:76–87. Other volumes with colonial sources are Andrew M. Davis, ed., *Colonial Currency Reprints, 1682–1751* (New York: Kelley, 1964) and Herman Krooss, ed., *Documentary History of Banking and Currency in the United States* (New York: McGraw-Hill, 1969). For information on paper money in China and England, see Lien-sheng Yang, *Money and Credit in China: A Short History* (Cambridge, Mass.: Harvard University Press, 1952); John Clapham, *The Bank of England: A History*, 2 vols. (Cambridge: Cambridge University Press, 1945); and Emanuel Coppieteis, *English Bank Note Circulation, 1694–1954* (The Hague: Louvain Institute, 1955).

Paper money is assessed in Roger Weiss, "The Issue of Paper Money in the American Colonies, 1720–1774," *Journal of Economic History* (December 1970), pp. 770–85; Weiss, "The Colonial Monetary Standard of Massachusetts," *Economic History Review*, (1974), 27:577–92; E. James Ferguson, "Currency Finance: An Interpretation of the Colonial Monetary Practices," *William and Mary Quarterly* (April 1953), pp. 153–80; and M. L. Burstein, "Colonial

Currency and Contemporary Monetary Theory: A Review Article,"
Explorations in Entreprenurial History (Spring 1966), pp. 220–33.
Two studies which focus on the origin of paper money emissions are
Andrew Davis, *Currency and Banking in the Providence of Massa-
chusetts Bay* (New York: Macmillan Co., 1901) and Richard Lester,
"Currency Issues to Overcome Depressions in Pennsylvania, 1723 and
1729," *Journal of Political Economy* (June 1963), pp. 324–75. A use-
ful review of the land banks is Theodore Thayer, "The Land Bank
System in the American Colonies," *Journal of Economic History*
(Spring 1953), pp. 145–59.

Several articles focus on the Currency Act of 1764; see Jack P.
Greene and Richard Jellison, "The Currency Act of 1764 in Imperial-
Colonial Relations, 1764–1776," *William and Mary Quarterly*,
(1961), 18:485–518; Robert Weir, "North Carolina's Reaction to the
Currency Act of 1764," *North Carolina Historical Review* (Spring
1963), pp. 183–99; and Joseph Ernst, "The Currency Act Repeal
Movement: A Study of Imperial Politics and Revolutionary Crisis,
1764–1769," *William and Mary Quarterly* (April 1968), pp. 177–
211. Another valuable article is Richard Sheridan, "The British
Credit Crisis of 1772 and the American Colonies," *Journal of Economic History* (June 1960), pp. 161–86.

Extensive data on the relative values of colonial monies is found in
John McCusker, *Money and Exchange in Europe and America,
1600–1775* (Chapel Hill: University of North Carolina Press, 1978).
For an analysis of the demand for money in sixteenth-century Spain,
see Dennis Flynn, "A New Perspective on the Spanish Price Revolution: The Monetary Approach to the Balance of Payments," *Explorations in Economic History*, (1978), 15:388–406.

Two new articles on the colonial monetary system are Robert Craig
West, "Money in the Colonial American Economy," *Economic In-
quiry* (January 1978), pp. 1–15, and John R. Hanson, "Money in the
Colonial American Economy: An Extension," *ibid.* (April 1979), pp.
281–86.

CHAPTER VII

TAXES AND POLITICS

THE level of taxation in the colonies was extremely low. The rates rarely, and only periodically, approached 20 percent of those prevailing in England. Few organized governments taxed their people so lightly in the seventeenth and eighteenth centuries. The colonists soon became accustomed to minimal taxation, and by the late colonial period they viewed low taxes as almost a birthright. Until 1764, the British had inadvertently encouraged this attitude, for Parliament had not only asked for little colonial revenue for over one hundred years, it had also regularly sent substantial taxes from the pockets of Englishmen overseas to finance a series of military campaigns on the North American continent. With their defense costs largely subsidized by the mother country, and without a sitting monarch, an idle aristocracy, or a large court establishment to support, the colonies incurred modest governmental expenses at the provincial level. Since the overall financial arrangements were quite favorable to the thirteen colonies, it is easy to understand why, after 1760, they attempted to maintain the status quo in Anglo-American relations.

Whether the independence movement had fundamentally economic or political origins has been the subject of scholarly debate for generations. The emphasis has shifted from one interpretation to another, depending upon the outlook of our most respected historians and the mode of historical analysis in vogue. The aim here is not to mediate that scholarly debate, although one side of the argument is tested and a tentative judgment offered. Because this chapter focuses almost exclusively on economic factors, many readers might reasonably assume at the outset that the author leans heavily toward an economic interpretation. That, however, is not the case; indeed, my review of the financial evidence has led me to downplay, but not eliminate, the importance of economic factors relative to the role of ideological conviction and the quest for political autonomy.

Many historians, however, are not so willing to dismiss economic forces and the issue of taxation. Several scholars argue that the rising rate of domestic taxation in the larger cities over the course of the eighteenth century was a source of urban discontent and may have contributed to the new political activism of artisans and common laborers in the 1760s and 1770s. In his recent book *The Urban Crucible*, Gary B. Nash points out that the amount of taxes paid by individual taxpayers during the Seven Years War rose rapidly; from 1750–54 to 1760–64 the tax burden increased 70 percent in New York, 80 percent in Boston, and 250 percent in Philadelphia. Although the tax burden had dropped back to prewar levels in Boston and New York by the 1770s, it failed to decline in Philadelphia. Nash believes that the rising level of taxes in the northern cities, the increasing incidences of poverty, and the stagnation of incomes for many artisans were, in combination, important parts of the calculations by which the colonists embarked upon a dual revolution to sever the colonial connection and internally reform their societies. Although I do not find his general argument compelling, it nonetheless represents an alternative viewpoint on a crucial issue.

Irrespective of their views about underlying causation, most historians have agreed that the movement for independence had economic precipitants. The strongly negative reaction to a proposed series of increases in imperial taxes, with further rises anticipated, was the catalyst that unified and mobilized a diverse group of mainland colonies.

DOMESTIC TAXES

In normal years, colonial legislatures voted taxes for a very limited number of government services. Salaries for the appointed governor, for a few judges, and in some provinces for the recognized clergy, plus compensation for their own legislative expenses, were typically major items in the annual budget. In colonies with outstanding government debts in the form of circulating paper money, a partial retirement sometimes made a heavy claim on revenues. In Massachusetts from 1765 to 1774, the average yearly expenditures were only £27,000 ($1.8 million), while New Hampshire spent just £2,000 ($130,000) in 1772. The costs of road maintenance, poor relief, and other incidentals were generally left to the counties and towns. Although the data remains sketchy, some evidence suggests that tax collections at the local level may have rivaled or exceeded provincial taxes in many areas, especially in the larger towns and cities.

By the late colonial era, per capita taxes at the provincial level generally ranged from 2 to 4 shillings, with 3 shillings ($9.75) a rough average. These taxes represented no more than 1.5 percent of estimated per capita incomes. In England, by comparison, the national tax rate ranged from 12 to 18 shillings ($40–$60) and represented from 5 to 7.5 percent of per capita incomes.

Each colony employed differing methods of taxing its inhabitants, and over the decades legislatures frequently shifted the emphasis from one tax to another. In the only comprehensive study of provincial taxes, Robert Becker has demonstrated the great variety of colonial revenue systems in the period after 1763. Except for poll (head) taxes and import taxes on slaves, the techniques of taxation are familiar today. As shown in Table 7.1, taxes were applied to land, livestock, inventories, liquor, imports and exports, and mercantile profits, including interest income.

Certain taxes were progressive and others basically regressive. In this era, property holding was considered a reliable indicator of yearly income. As a consequence, taxes based on assessed values of land, improvements, personal property, and inventories were relatively progressive, because they normally reflected a person's ability to pay. One method assessors used to determine land values was to make estimates on the basis of the rents paid by tenants on comparable plots in the same region. In England, land taxes were stated as a percentage of each £100 in rents or potential rental income. In the colonies, the

TABLE 7.1. Types of Domestic Taxes, 1763-1775

Land—unimproved	Rhode Island, Pennsylvania
Land—assessed value	Massachusetts, Rhode Island, Connecticut, Pennsylvania, New Jersey
Land—per acre	Virginia, Maryland, South Carolina, Georgia
Other property—assessed	Massachusetts, New Jersey, South Carolina
Excise—liquor, etc.	New Hampshire, New York, Maryland, Virginia, North Carolina
Import—finished goods	Pennsylvania, New York, Georgia
Import-slaves	New York, Maryland, South Carolina
Export—tobacco	Maryland, Virginia
Merchant profits	Massachusetts, New Hampshire, Pennsylvania, Connecticut, Rhode Island, South Carolina
Poll—flat	Maryland, Virginia, North Carolina
Poll—linked to wealth	Connecticut, Massachusetts, Rhode Island
Poll—discriminatory toward free blacks	South Carolina, Georgia

SOURCE: Robert A. Becker, "The Politics of Taxation in America, 1763-1783" (Ph.D. dissertation, University of Wisconsin, 1971).

most progressive tax systems included levies on unimproved, wilderness tracts held for speculation; while the more regressive systems, all in the south, taxed farmland strictly by the acre, irrespective of its productive value.

Poll taxes applied to males over a certain age, often sixteen, fell most heavily on families with low incomes. Their regressive impact was often modified, however, by increasing the poll tax rate in line with the value of other taxable property, which was the system followed in Connecticut and Rhode Island. In the south, a greater share of the burden was shifted to slaveholders, since they usually became liable for additional head taxes on all slaves and servants over twelve, females as well as males. Georgia and South Carolina used poll taxes for purposes of racial discrimination; they imposed them exclusively on free blacks.

Other items produced tax revenues. Several colonies taxed the vices, by charging import duties on rum and wine plus excise taxes on domestic liquors. In the Chesapeake region, export taxes on tobacco were an important source of revenue, with those growers shipping the largest number of hogsheads progressively incurring the largest share of taxes. In some provinces, legislators sought tax revenue from business "faculties," by which they meant the incomes of merchants from trade and money lending. In Massachusetts, the tax rate on incomes from business activities was set at 5 percent in 1773. Finally, as discussed in the last chapter, some colonies imposed a tax burden in a disguised manner by forcing the holders of paper currency to suffer steady depreciation.

The New England colonies generally had the most progressive tax structures. Land and property taxes were based on assessed values, which shifted more of the burden to the wealthier citizens. Northern merchants were usually subject to income levies; and poll taxes, when applied, were often linked to property holding. Perhaps because South Carolina also had a major port city in Charleston, Becker found that it was one southern colony with a tax system similar to New England's. The only colony with a consistently regressive tax structure in the eighteenth century was North Carolina, where the legislature relied heavily on flat poll taxes and excise taxes on liquor for revenue. The other southern and middle colonies employed a mixture of taxes with progressive and regressive features.

In the colonies with major port cities, legislative battles over the assignment of regional tax quotas were frequent. It was common practice to assign counties and towns the responsibility for collecting a fixed portion of a colony's revenues. Boston, Providence, New York, Philadelphia, and Charleston complained constantly that they bore a disproportionate share of provincial taxes. Usually underrepresented in the legislatures, the ports' residents often fought, for example, to prevent the assessment of their property at values closer to market prices than corresponding assessments in the rural areas. Philadelphia paid 43 percent of the provincial property taxes between 1763 and 1775. In South Carolina, the only place where land taxes were assessed ad valorem rather than per acre was in Charleston.

The port cities also sought tax relief because of the relatively high cost of government services at the local level. Poor relief had become a large item in city budgets by the late colonial era. In the 1760s, Boston allocated up to 60 percent of its local taxes for charity; the city spent £3,057 ($198,700) on poor relief in 1769 and £3,355 ($218,000) in 1773. Charleston's representatives complained about the number of indigents who flocked into the city, and they badgered the province to assume greater responsibility for poor relief. The belief, widespread today, that modern American cities, under the strong influence of sympathetic liberals, were the first to allocate a substantial portion of their tax funds for various welfare programs is contradicted by the performance of the colonial port cities.

Although the legislative contests between rural and urban residents were sometimes lengthy and acrimonious, the maneuvering for advantage and the rhetoric displayed in debates over tax policies should not obscure the point that, for the most part, little money was really at stake. Tax rates were so low in all the colonies that no class or region was unduly burdened. Even in port cities with above-average local rates, the net tax burden was rarely more than 4 or 5 percent of family income, and in rural counties the figures were much lower. In a study of the family budgets of common laborers in Philadelphia in the 1770s, Billy Smith estimated that taxes accounted for about 5 percent of annual income. In the 1980s, U.S. citizens commonly pay up to 30 percent of their income in taxes for government services. By modern standards, colonial taxes were almost unbelievably light.

IMPERIAL TAXES

Leaving aside all constitutional questions and the institutional mechanism for colonial representation in Parliament, from a financial standpoint one can readily empathize with the Exchequers of the British Treasury in their quest for an American tax revenue. At the close of the Seven Years War (French and Indian) in 1763, Britain had accumulated an enormous national debt of more than

£135,000,000 ($8.8 billion) plus continuing defense costs in newly won Canada, along the midwestern frontier, and at sea in the North Atlantic. The expense of maintaining these military forces overseas was over £400,000 ($26 million) annually. Tax rates in England had been high in 1755 and went higher during the war; the land tax jumped from 10 percent of assessed value to 20 percent, and excise taxes were raised across the board. Lance Davis and Robert Huttenback estimated that British taxes yielded about £1 ($65) per capita over the period from 1770 to 1775, or about 6 percent of net national product. The British tax rate was almost certainly the highest in the Western world. Meanwhile, prior to 1764, the colonial contribution to meeting these war and defense costs in North America was virtually nil.

Until the 1760s, Parliament had reserved the right to disallow the acts of the colonial legislatures, but it had failed to seek a steady tax revenue from the mainland colonies. Only the Virginians, who continued to pay quitrents, and old form of feudal dues, in amounts up to £5,000 ($325,000) annually until Independence, made any regular contributions to the imperial coffers, and those sums were trifling. Maryland's quitrents went to the proprietor, Lord Baltimore, rather than to Parliament. Quitrents due in other colonies were rarely collected.

The series of Navigation Acts applied to colonial trade after 1650 had placed duties on the importation of certain foreign products, but the aim was to constrain the pattern of commerce, not to generate imperial revenues. Thomas Barrow estimated that the cost of collecting these duties on the mainland often exceeded the amounts received. The Molasses Act of 1733 raised the duty on imports from the French and Spanish islands in the Caribbean to 6 pence ($1.62) per gallon; the intention was to halt or significantly curtail the foreign molasses trade. But, the colonists evaded the royal customs collectors or settled with them for a fraction of the total due; in Boston, one-tenth was reportedly the standard rate for looking the other way. When these duties were established, no one in the colonies had raised serious questions about the absence of colonial representation in Parliament. Until the mid-eighteenth-century, the legislatures were still relatively inexperienced at running their own affairs and were less bold in asserting their political autonomy.

The Navigation Acts had, of course, placed a burden on the colonial economy. But it came in the form of lost opportunities for additional profits—especially the direct sale of enumerated goods to the European continent. As discussed at greater length in chapter 2, the indirect burden on the colonies was slightly more than the benefits accruing to them from British defense spending in the late colonial period. Few contemporaries were in a position to make even tentative estimates of the opportunity costs associated with membership in the British Empire, however. In the colonies, Daniel Dulaney, a Maryland lawyer and ardent pamphleteer, calculated that restrictions on the tobacco trade alone reduced grower's profits by about £270,000 ($17.5 million) in 1765. Dulany's calculations were fairly accurate and erred, if at all, on the conservative side. Such arguments fell on deaf ears in the Exchequer's office, for even if true, these hypothetical "costs" made no tangible contribution to imperial tax revenues.

The colonists were not merely successful in avoiding direct imperial taxation; they also succeeded in gaining substantial reimbursements from Parliament for funds expended on numerous military campaigns against French and Spanish outposts or settlements. Until 1763, the British, the latecomers to the New World, were engaged in a struggle for empire on the North American continent with European rivals. The colonies were intelligent enough to use this British thirst for military and political empire to their own advantage. In return for firm promises from Parliament to reimburse them fully at a later date, the colonies frequently agreed to recruit soldiers locally and to supply them throughout a military campaign. In many colonies, the governors and their legislative allies were anxious to volunteer their aid under these favorable conditions, or even instigate hostilities, for the profits from war contracts were one of the few financially rewarding opportunities available to government officials and their friends and relatives.

The system was doubly advantageous, because in the long run the English taxpayer footed most of the bill. Parliamentary ministers were not familiar with the financial capabilities of the colonies and acquiring accurate information from overseas was slow and difficult. When the colonists grieved about their own allegedly high taxes and limited resources, crown ministers, ignorant of the real situation, felt they had little choice but to aquiesce to demands for complete reimbursement, since the possible expansion of the overseas empire and the defeat of a rival power took precedent over more mundane considerations like taxation.

In the period from 1757 to 1767 alone, Parliament sent over £800,000 ($52 million) to the thirteen colonies to reimburse them for expenses incurred during the victorious French and Indian War. The legislatures used this largesse in many cases to lower provincial tax rates, which fell everywhere from 1765 to 1775. By 1770, most of the colonies were virtually debt free, while English taxpayers were saddled with interest payments of £5 million ($325 million) annually to service a swollen national debt. Ironically, by fulfilling its earlier pledges of reimbursement, Parliament had unwittingly reinforced the colonists' belief in their general immunity to a sustained burden of high taxes.

When the English government, after decades of indifference and neglect, finally began to reassess its colonial policies in the early 1760s, the costs of maintaining a militarily secure North American empire were uppermost in the minds of the crown ministers. They were resigned to accepting the expenditures on the past war as a "sunk" cost, irretrievable and now irrelevant. But the continuing peacetime expenses were viewed in a much different light. Based primarily on the advice of the British military commander in North America, Lord Jeffery Amherst, the ministry had decided to station about 10,000 troops overseas.

The costs of colonial defense soon rose to over £400,000 ($26 million) per year. Excluding interest payments on the national debt, these sums accounted for about 12 percent of Parliament's operating budget and were more than twice the amounts spent on North American defense prior to 1755. The thirteen mainland colonies, the ministry assumed, were the prime beneficiaries of this British military presence, but, as in the past, they were contributing nothing to its upkeep. A colonial revenue to offset at least some of these ongoing expenses therefore seemed in order.

The first act designed specifically to raise a colonial revenue actually lowered the duty on foreign molasses and wine. The prohibitive duty of 6 pence ($1.62) per gallon on molasses imported from the French and Spanish islands in the Caribbean dropped to only 3 pence ($.81) per gallon. The rate on wine shipped though Britain came down too. This 1764 law signaled a major shift away from the strategy of using high duties in the colonies almost exclusively for protectionism—with the beneficiaries in this instance being influential British investors in the Caribbean. The new policy called for more modest rates that, given an enlarged volume of trade, might generate substantial tax revenues. In 1766, the molasses duty came down again to merely one penny ($.27) per gallon, but it now applied to all molasses entering the colonies, British as well as foreign. The two reductions in duties on molasses were expected to reduce the incidence of smuggling, previously rampant, and to stimulate more trade.

To handle the anticipated larger volume of commerce and to tighten the enforcement of imperial regulations in general, Parliament also decided in 1764 to reorganize and upgrade the colonial customs service. Except for the royal governors and a few high-ranking military officers, these poorly paid customs officers were the only visible representatives of the British government in the colonies. While some colonial leaders were apprehensive about the language in the preamble of the tariff-revision act, which proclaimed forthrightly the goal of raising an overseas revenue, and others were suspicious about the greater degree of imperial control, they were in no position to protest too loudly. Duties on imports clearly fell within the scope of the long-standing navigation laws. Moreover, the tax rates on wine and molasses had been lowered rather than raised, which left few grounds for complaint.

The ministry headed by George Grenville thus made an auspicious start toward producing a steady colonial revenue in 1764. The precedents for taxing foreign commerce were well established in the colonies. Collected from merchants when goods entered port, the tax burden was passed along to consumers indirectly in the form of higher prices. The tax revenues anticipated from this alteration in the duty on molasses were largely realized. In the period from 1768 to 1771, for example, around 3.5 million gallons of molasses entered through the customs houses annually and generated duties of £14,000 ($910,000) yearly. These amounts alone were sufficient to convert the operations of the customs service on the mainland, even after its expansion, from a perennial financial loser into a slightly profitable government bureau. But the net revenues from the molasses and wine duties combined hardly covered a fraction of the military budget for North America.

Seeking additional sources of revenue, the Grenville ministry settled on a stamp tax in 1765. A common feature of the English tax system, stamp duties applied to a host of legal and government documents, including wills, licenses, and deeds, to name a few—plus miscellaneous items, like newspaper advertisements, playing cards, and dice. The aim was to raise roughly £40,000 ($2.6 million) in the colonies or about 10 percent of the yearly costs of defense.

The Stamp Act marked a significant departure from previous Parliamentary behavior, and it produced a loud outcry in the colonies. Unlike the duties on imports, the stamp levies were not hidden in the prices of consumer goods. They were instead highly visible taxes. An atypical form of colonial taxation, the stamp fees were certain to catch the attention of the average citizen.

An internal tax was also unprecedented in imperial relations. Many legislative leaders in the colonies called them plainly unconstitutional, because their enactment violated the uniquely British political principle of no taxation without the presence of adequate representation in Parliament to affirm the consent of the voters. Some legislators in 1765 distinguished between Parliament's prerogative to vote external taxes and the alleged illegality of other internal taxes, but the majority were becoming increasingly opposed to any imperial taxation whatsoever, or at least to any increases in existing levels. Few Americans bothered to consider the fact that implementation of the Stamp Act threatened to cost the average taxpayer no more than 5 pence ($1.35) a year, or less than two-tenths of one percent of per capita incomes.

Instead they organized a protest movement. The colonists terrorized or intimidated the appointed tax collectors and forced them either to resign their positions or to agree not to perform their assigned duties. Nine of the thirteen colonies sent representatives to a hastily called Congress in New York to coordinate strategies. It issued a declaration protesting the passage of the Stamp Act, in particular, and the enactment of tax laws without representation, in general. The principle of the matter was now at stake; it was more than just a question of money.

An intense lobbying effort was directed at English merchants trading extensively with the colonies. The merchants were expected to assist in the coordinated movement to gain repeal of the stamp tax, for if that movement failed, the colonies threatened to continue indefinitely the organized boycott of English imports. The colonists soon learned, like the Arab countries in the 1970s, that an economic boycott could become a powerful political tool.

Faced with such extreme and completely unexpected hostility, and with the surprising cohesiveness of the colonial opposition, Parliament backed down and repealed the Stamp Act in 1766. The way was eased when Benjamin Franklin explicitly assured the House of Commons, in person, that his countrymen objected solely to internal taxes, and not to traditional forms of external taxes on imports. Whether Franklin was badly misinformed or deliberately mislead Parliament to gain temporary advantage is uncertain, but his expression of colonial sentiments was grossly inaccurate, as Edmund and Helen Morgan demonstrated in their brilliant analysis of the Stamp Act controversy.

Determined to reassert its legislative superiority and now convinced that the colonists had no constitutional objections to further increases in import duties, Parliament looked about for other revenue opportunities. A change of ministries brought Charles Townshend in as Chancellor of the Exchequer. A former member of the colonial Board of Trade, Townshend was much more familiar with overseas affairs then his predecessors.

His experience had indicated that the colonial governors were generally much too dependent on the goodwill of their supposedly subordinate legislatures. This happened, he reasoned, because those legislatures normally had control of their governors' salaries. The governors' divided allegiance on so many vital issues was thus easily understood. The failure of Parliament to assume the financial responsibility for these salaries—and to give thereby the governors a measure of independence from local political pressure—had been, in Townshend's mind, a major blunder in imperial affairs—a prime example of false economy. A portion of any new overseas revenues would go, he planned, to pay the salaries of the royal governors. The cost was relatively modest, probably less than £20,000 ($1.3 million). Given the realities of colonial politics, however, this was one expense the legislatures did not wish to surrender.

In late 1766 and early 1767, Townshend reviewed a series of new tax proposals for the colonies. Meanwhile, the vote in Parliament to lower the English land tax by 25 percent, a bill he had opposed, cost the new Chancellor of the Exchequer about £500,000 ($32.5 million), and made the search for alternative sources of income even more compelling. For a time, Townshend considered a plan for a land-bank office for all the colonies, with the interest revenues accuring to the imperial coffers. The plan had circulated in London for years and had been recommended by Benjamin Franklin and other colonial agents as an alternative to the stamp tax in 1765. The proposal appeared to have considerable merit, since the colonies were simultaneously pressing for a liberalization in the terms of the Currency Act of 1764. The issuance of paper money through Parliamentary loan offices might even be welcomed overseas and might be the ideal solution for two outstanding issues: money and taxes.

But for a combination of reasons, Townshend decided to lay aside the land-office proposal and to concentrate instead on raising the duties on other American imports. Several factors probably influenced his decision. A Parliamentary land bank and a single paper-currency system would link together more closely the economies of the thirteen colonies, and the outcome of the coordinated protest against the stamp tax had revealed that too much economic unity might carry with it serious political dangers. Second, many Englishmen still had reservations about the propriety of paper money as a circulating medium. After passing a series of acts restricting its usage, the most recent in 1764, Parliament might feel reluctant to reverse policy so suddenly. Finally, Townshend may have feared that the colonists might interpret the collection of interest income as a form of internal taxation and respond with another protest movement. Based on Franklin's assurances, new taxes on imports seemed less controversial and therefore the safer alternative.

Townshend finally recommended new duties on glass, paint leads, paper, and tea. The aim was to generate about £40,000 ($2.6 million)—the same figure as the earlier stamp tax—in new revenues immediately, with other increases planned in subsequent years. The amount represented about 10 percent of British defense expenditures in North America. The bill passed Parliament with hardly a dissent, not even from the colonies' staunchest allies in the constitutional battle over the stamp tax.

The reaction in the colonies to the new Townshend duties was comparable to the response to the stamp tax. Having challenged and successfully undermined the most recent British attempt to increase taxes, the colonists were disposed to try again. The arguments about the absence of representation in Parliament were revived—with no distinctions between the implementation of internal and external taxes,

Franklin's remarks notwithstanding. The constitutional issue was in the forefront of colonial minds, and it extended not merely to taxes but had escalated into queries about the power of Parliament over colonial affairs in general.

To combat the Townshend duties, the colonists relied most heavily on the proven record of economic coercion. A boycott of all English imports was quickly organized, and watchdog committees of citizens held shopkeepers in the larger cities in line. Since few British goods were necessities, the boycott meant inconveniences for some consumers, but few colonists lost their livelihood or suffered serious declines in income, except a few merchants in the major ports. The Americans were, by this point, an aroused and determined people.

The volume of business lost by British merchants closely associated with the colonial trade was staggering. In 1768 and 1769 combined, the figure rose to over £1 million ($65 million) in sales foregone. The sum literally dwarfed the meager amount of £2,700 ($175,500) collected from the Townshend duties in 1770. The economic realities of the situation dictated again that Parliament knuckle under, and it finally conceded defeat by rescinding all the Townshend duties—except one. The tax on tea was retained as a symbol of Parliamentary authority. But for all practical purposes, Parliament had thrown in the towel in 1770. The effort to establish a permanent colonial revenue to offset a major portion of the costs of defending North America had failed. In short, the one economic issue driving a wedge between the mother country and her mainland colonies had been largely resolved. Only the matter of political autonomy remained outstanding.

The colonists resented the continuation of the tax on tea, but they begrudgingly paid it. After falling to a low of 108,600 pounds in 1770, tea imports rebounded sharply in 1771 to 359,000 pounds and remained steady over the next two years. In the period from 1771 to 1773, the customs service collected duties of £34,000 ($2.2 million) yearly, mainly on molasses, wine, sugar, and tea. These sums amply covered the expenses of operating the customs houses and provided funds to pay the salaries of the governors of Massachusetts and New York, judges of the Admiralty Courts, and a few other imperial officials. Some of the monies even became available for the royal navy patrolling in the North Atlantic.

The final episode linked to the tea tax occurred in late 1773. The East India Company, a large English trading firm closely tied to the government, found itself in serious financial difficulties. The firm had enormous holdings of tea in its English warehouses, and in an effort to save the company from bankruptcy, Parliament granted it a monopoly on tea sales to the colonies. Hoping to forestall a possible charge of financial exploitation, Parliament adjusted the tea regulations and tax rates in England so that tea prices overseas would drop, even after the payment of the existing colonial tea duty.

This effort to rescue the East India Company and to give colonial consumers the benefit of lower prices went awry, however. A small group of militant colonists, still angered by the tea tax, seized this opportunity to inflame public opinion. They focused on the monopoly issue in particular, with unsupported claims that the East India Company had plans to undermine the entire mercantile community and obtain exclusive rights to all colonial commerce, not merely tea. Circulars asserted that the real motive behind the whole scheme was to force the colonies to recognize the legitimacy of the existing tea tax. Since Americans had been paying that tax for over two years, the latter charge was overblown. But in the politically charged colonial atmosphere, the economic logic of the situation was totally lost.

On the night of December 16, 1773, the Boston Tea Party took place. Tea valued at £9,000 ($585,000) was destroyed by 30 to 40 men in a well-executed, three-hour operation. Parliament promptly closed the port of Boston. The First Continental Congress met in September 1774; fighting erupted at Lexington and Concord in April 1775; and the final movement for independence was well under way.

How important were economic forces in causing the American revolt? In the five years prior to the signing of the Declaration of Independence, the British imposed no new taxes. Parliament gave little serious consideration to alternative revenue proposals for the colonies. The retention of the tea tax in 1770 was strictly a face-saving device. The colonies had demonstrated twice within a five year period the power of the boycott. Parliament was ready to settle for the status quo, including the assumption of over 90 percent of the defense expenditures in North America.

The remaining imperial taxes were hardly burdensome. The Virginia quitrents contributed around £4,000 ($260,000) yearly, and customs duties grossed £34,000 ($2.2 million), but they netted only £18,000 ($1.2 million) after expenses. The imperial tax burden was 4 pence ($1.08) per capita—a negligible portion of family income even in the eighteenth century, no more than a thousandth of one percent. Meanwhile, domestic tax rates continued to decline after 1765; by the 1770s, provincial taxes had fallen below 3 shillings ($9.75) per head or just over one percent of income in some colonies. The colonial rhetoric about the heavy burden of existing taxes was mostly that—rhetoric with little substance.

Taxes were a major unresolved issue in Anglo-American relations only in the period from 1765 to 1770. They were the surface topic around which most political and constitutional arguments centered. Doubting the sincerity of colonial statements about the necessity of representation in the taxation process, historians have often noted the colonies' acceptance of the revision of the molasses duty in 1764. The molasses tax was, however, a special situation. This tax on molasses imports had been in effect for over a century, and the adjustment was downward to one-half and later one-sixth of the former rate. No American representatives in Parliament, had they existed, could have objected strongly to that form of tax revision.

The stamp tax and later Townshend duties were different matters altogether, because they proposed to increase colonial tax rates. Although designed to raise only 10 to 15 percent of Parliament's annual defense budget in North America, many contemporaries and subsequent scholars noted that these new taxes were only a beginning.

More revenue acts were certain to follow, as Grenville and Townshend had clearly intimated in speeches to the House of Commons. According to this line of argument, the colonial tax revenues might soon approach the per capita levels in England, and thereafter exceed them. Within a few years, the colonies would become major contributors to the allegedly bloated and corrupt British government, headed by a lavish monarch who maintained a host of pensioners and other parasites. To avoid this outcome, revolt and independence were justified and, moreover, easily explained.

The hypothesis that the political separation had economic origins rests heavily then on the estimate of what was likely to happen at some undetermined point in the future. The alleged intent of Parliament to raise taxes higher and higher provides the main evidence. In other circumstances, historians have considered such speculative evidence extremely weak, but in the context of American independence it seems to have survived and thrived.

In this case, the economic argument is doubly suspect, because it is questionable on its own terms. Even if such predictions had proved accurate and tax increases had become a reality in subsequent decades, political separation in the 1760s on the basis of anticipated future costs would have been financially premature. Furthermore, even if the burden associated with the Navigation Acts is included in the calculations, the overall cost of participation in the British Empire was no more than 5 shillings ($16.25) per head. Taxes would have had to jump over 150 percent in the colonies to reach a per capita equalization figure with England, according to a recent study by Joseph Reid. Borrowing from modern business techniques for appraising investment alternatives, we can also calculate that the "present value" of any future tax payments, using a modest discount rate of 8 percent, were very low in 1765, when based on the steady implementation of British intentions over a twenty-year period. Long before the development of sophisticated investment analysis techniques, the colonists knew very well that a tax dollar avoided in 1765 was worth considerably more than the same amount paid, if at all, at some indefinite date in the future. The independence movement came, in sum, a generation too early for an economic explanation of the origins to account largely for its occurrence.

As one part of their new research on the economic costs and benefits associated with modern political empires, Lance Davis and Robert Huttenback examined the British experience in North America after 1750. They found that the course of events in the thirteen colonies was consistent with the normal pattern elsewhere: few of the colonial ventures of the Western European nations proved financially beneficial to the mother country. With the possible exception of the colonization of India, British overseas ventures consistently cost more to defend and administer than they were worth. The maintenance of an empire in North America during the eighteenth century saddled English taxpayers with an enormous burden of war debts and escalating defense expenditures. From a purely economic standpoint, Davis and Huttenback speculated that Britain was probably a "victor" in defeat, for, after independence, U.S. taxes rose precipitously. From 1792 to 1811, U.S. per capita tax rates were over 10 times higher than those levied by the British from 1765 to 1775.

The economic tactics from 1765 to 1770 had significant implications for future political action. The colonies had become a large market for English goods over the course of the eighteenth century. The extent of British dependency on American markets was revealed in its vulnerability to the trade boycott. The colonies had found a powerful economic and political weapon to use against a nation heavily reliant on international commerce for its prosperity. Almost forty years later, Presidents Thomas Jefferson and James Madison adopted a similar strategy of economic coercion in the years preceding the War of 1812. The trade embargo was less successful in the first decade of the nineteenth century, but its potential nonetheless remained. In the 1970s, the Arab nations imposed an oil embargo against the United States, and the tactic was widely deplored. Ironically, a leader in the innovative use of economic coercion had become its chief victim almost two centuries later.

When the crown ministers tried in the early 1760s to increase sev-
eralfold colonial taxes and to generate a revenue to offset somewhat
the high cost of defending North America, the colonies protested
strongly. The rate of increase was very rapid, given the very low base
of imperial taxation in prior decades. The British aimed initially at
raising perhaps 15 percent of their overseas defense expenditures. But
the colonists found these new taxes unacceptable in practice and on
principle. The confrontation over imperial taxes escalated into debates
over constitutional issues like representation in Parliament and the future role of the colonies in the empire.

In conclusion, we have tested the hypothesis that economic differences between the colonies and the mother country were in large
part responsible for the final political separation in the 1770s. It is not
a convincing argument. The degree of economic regulation and the
level of imperial taxation were not significant causes of the War for
Independence, for they had little real impact on the colonies. At the
same time, we have not examined as closely the thesis that economic
and social rivalries among merchants, artisans, and common laborers
may have contributed to stirring up revolutionary sentiment in the
major port cities of Boston, New York, and Philadelphia. This line of
argument may ultimately prove fruitful, but I remain skeptical. Having discounted heavily theories about the economic origins of the independence movement, we must look to other explanations—ideological,
political, social—for the motivations behind the independence movement.

BIBLIOGRAPHICAL ESSAYS

The best source on colonial taxation is, surprisingly, an unpublished
dissertation by Robert A. Becker, entitled "The Politics of Taxation in
America, 1763–1783," which was completed at the University of Wisconsin in 1971 and is now available from University Microfilms in

Ann Arbor, Michigan. Becker has published "Revolution and Reform: An Interpretation of Southern Taxation, 1763 to 1783," *William and Mary Quarterly* (July 1975), pp. 417–42.

The collection of imperial taxes is covered in Thomas Barrow, *Trade and Empire: The British Customs Service in Colonial America, 1660–1775* (Cambridge, Mass.: Harvard University Press, 1967). Two other useful books are Beverly Bond, *The Quit-Rent System in the American Colonies* (New Haven, Conn.: Yale University Press, 1919) and Margaret G. Myers, *A Financial History of the United States* (New York: Columbia University Press, 1970). A recent article on the lower south is Alan P. Watson, "The Quitrent System in Royal South Carolina," *William and Mary Quarterly* (April 1976), pp. 183–211. For information on taxation in England and on the continent, see Stephen Dowell, *A History of Taxation and Taxes in England,* 6 vols. (1884; reprinted, New York: Kelley, 1965); and Carlo Cippola, *Before the Industrial Revolution: European Society and Economy, 1000–1700* (New York: Norton, 1976), p. 47.

On the tax revisions and political controversies during the last quarter century before the break with Britain, see Bernhard Knollenberg, *Origin of the American Revolution, 1759–1766* (New York: Free Press, 1965); Knollenberg, *Growth of the American Revolution, 1766–1775* (New York: Free Press, 1975); Edmund and Helen Morgan, *The Stamp Act Crisis: Prologue to Revolution* (Chapel Hill: University of North Carolina Press, 1953); and Jack P. Greene, *The Quest for Power: The Lower Houses of Assembly in the Southern Royal Colonies, 1689–1776* (Chapel Hill: University of North Carolina Press, 1963). For a description of the tax system in one colony, see Marvin Kay, "The Payment of Provincial and Local Taxes in North Carolina, 1748–1771," *William and Mary Quarterly* (April 1969), pp. 218–40.

The events after 1766 are covered in P. D. G. Thomas, "Charles Townshend and American Taxation in 1767," *English Historical Review* (January 1968), pp. 33–51; Robert Chaffin, "The Townshend

Acts of 1767," *William and Mary Quarterly* (January 1970), pp. 90–121; and Benjamin Labaree, *The Boston Tea Party* (New York: Oxford University Press, 1964).

For a different interpretation of the importance of economic forces, see Joseph Reid, Jr., "Economic Burden: Spark to the American Revolution," *Journal of Economic History* (March 1978), pp. 81–100; Marc Egnal and Joseph Ernst, "An Economic Interpretation of the American Revolution," *William and Mary Quarterly* (January 1972), pp. 3–32; and Gary Nash, *The Urban Crucible* (Cambridge, Mass.: Harvard University Press, forthcoming). Nash also shared with me his manuscript entitled "Taxation in the Northern Colonial Cities."

Lance Davis and Robert Huttenback place the events in colonial North America in a comparative perspective in a working paper prepared at the California Institute of Technology.

CHAPTER VIII

LIVING STANDARDS AND INCOME GROWTH

THE material standard of living enjoyed by the typical
white family unit in the thirteen mainland English colonies
was almost certainly the highest in the world by the 1770s.
Leaving aside regional variation, I have estimated median income per
capita for the free population at around £13 ($845); a typical family
of five lived quite satisfactorily on £65 ($4,225). By comparison, the
typical white family with 3.3 members in 1980 had an average income
of roughly $21,500. Living standards for the typical American thus
have risen about eightfold over the last two centuries. The incomes of
slaves—measured in food, clothing, housing, and other maintenance
costs—were probably around £7 ($455) per capita. The typical
member of a black family unit in 1980 had an income of approximately $3,300, which translates into a sevenfold improvement
since the colonial period.

Average incomes in the mother country in the eighteenth century
were probably somewhat below the figure for the free colonial population. The typical Englishman had an income of £10 ($650) to £12
($780). The colonists also had higher disposable incomes for the
purchase of goods and services, because taxes in the colonies (local to
imperial) were at least 75 percent below those prevailing in England.
As a result, the typical colonial family maintained a material standard
of living around one-fifth above its counterpart across the Atlantic
Ocean.

The accepted view of what level of income constitutes wealth or
poverty in America has changed radically over time. Colonial incomes,
high by the standards of the time, were about 50 percent lower than
the official poverty line established by the U.S. government for a farm
family of five members in 1979. Similarly, they were one-quarter

in the past and today, is the small amounts of protein in diets. The colonists ate large quantities of pork, beef, and poultry. In most areas the adult consumption was almost half a pound of protein-rich meat per day.

The food supplies available in the port cities were ample and varied. In a study of eighteenth-century Boston, Karen Friedmann found a surprisingly efficient system of food accumulation and distribution. Many city residents bought their bread from local bakers and willingly paid prices from 35 to 85 percent higher for wheat loaves than for corn or rye. Cattle was driven into town on foot, and the business of butchers flourished by mid-century. Friedmann estimated that Bostonians drank milk at two meals every day. For the most part, city residents lived on nutritionally sound diets, except perhaps during the winter months when the selection of food was limited. The typical urban family spent up to 50 percent of its income on food, with sizable meat supplies included in that total. Today, the average American family spends about 17 percent of its after-tax income on groceries, while the inhabitants of the world's poorest nations frequently devote up to 70 percent of their meager earnings to maintain an unvaried and almost meatless diet.

A new methodology for estimating the nutritional status of the colonists comes from an analysis of the average height of males entering the military in the eighteenth century. Kenneth Sokoloff and Georgia Villaflor studied the muster rolls of soldiers recruited to fight in the French and Indian War (1756–1763) and the War for Independence (1775–1783). They discovered that native-born Americans were surprisingly tall; indeed, the native-born group had already reached modern heights, or an average of about 5'8''. Scientific research has proven a direct correlation between the general level of nutrition plus the consumption of protein and final heights for individuals. Sokoloff and Villaflor's findings corroborate other evidence indicating that the colonials were avid meat eaters. Based on an analysis of the occupations listed by recruits, they found no significant difference in heights among farmers, artisans, common laborers, or social classes generally, which suggests that the diet of the lower class in the colonies was nutritionally sound. Southerners tended to be taller, but they may have been measured with their shoes on rather than in their stocking feet.

Sokoloff and Villaflor also found that colonial soldiers were normally two inches taller than recruits entering the service of the British Royal Marines. The existence of this differential suggests that colonial diets were more ample and varied than across the Atlantic. Since large meat consumption is typically a sign of high incomes in a developing economy, this factor reinforces the argument that living standards were higher in the colonies than in the mother country in the mid-eighteenth century.

In new research on the living standards of the lower class in Philadelphia in the mid-eighteenth-century, Billy Smith drew up a household budget covering food, rent, wood, and clothing for tailors, cordwainers (shoemakers), common laborers, and sailors. For the typical family of four (two adults, two children) in these occupational categories, the annual cost of food, including a half pound of meat daily plus milk, was around £31 ($2,015); rent varied from a low of £10 ($650) for laborers up to £22 ($1,430) for cordwainers and tailors; firewood for heating and cooking ran about £5 ($325), and clothing—including a pair of shoes, two shirts, one pair of pants or a skirt, and a cloth coat for each family member—cost around £8.5 ($550). Taxes added another £2 ($130) or £3 ($195). The normal budget for a lower-class family in Philadelphia was approximately £60 ($3,900), or £15 ($975) per capita. By eliminating meat from the diet, a family could cut its food budget by one-half, but it was still difficult to get by on much less than £35 ($2,275) to £40 ($2,600) per year. Fully employed males in these occupation groups could earn up to the following amounts: laborers—£60 ($3,900); sailor—£49 ($3,185); journeyman cordwainer—£58.5 ($3,800); master cordwainer—£74 ($4,800); journeyman tailor—£62.5 ($4,060); and master tailor—£100 ($6,500). Because of irregular employment patterns in these occupations, however, many families were pressed to maintain living standards without extra income from the part-time employment of wives and children. (Ironically, many American families today find themselves in a similar position, despite a median family income of over $20,000 in 1980.)

Smith characterized the lower classes in Philadelphia as living in very circumscribed material conditions and constantly threatened by the unpredictability of illness, seasonal unemployment, and general economic slowdowns. Despite the meagerness of their family incomes and the degree of vulnerability from a twentieth-century perspective, the colonial urban worker, nonetheless, experienced an unusually high standard of living for the eighteenth century and one still above the global median in 1980.

Differences in income and wealth distribution existed between regions and between rural and urban areas. New England had the lowest levels of white per capita income and wealth because of its rocky soils. Incomes in the four northernmost colonies were probably close to £11 ($715) per head, or about the same level as in the mother country. The monetary values of physical wealth included in probated estates in New England were lower than in the middle and southern colonies. Alice Hanson Jones, who has produced a series of masterful quantitative studies on the colonies, found the mean physical wealth of free adult wealth-holders in New England was £161 ($10,400) in 1774.* Median, or typical, wealth was £74 ($4,800); the top 5 percent of all estates held 32 percent of the region's wealth (table 8.1).

The middle colonies had the least concentrated distribution of wealth on the mainland. Median wealth was 80 percent of the mean figure of £189 ($12,300). The top 5 percent of all estates held only 24 percent of the region's wealth. Incomes in the middle region were around £13 ($845) per head, which was typical for the free population in all the colonies.

The southern colonies, with a large slave population, had the most unusual pattern of wealth and income distribution. Slaves held no

---

* All wealth data is from her book *American Colonial Wealth* (2d ed., 1978), assumption B. Estimates of *mean* incomes are based on the analysis in her new book *Wealth of a Nation To Be*. Estimates of median incomes are strictly my own, however; see Appendix.

TABLE 8.1. Total Physical Wealth, 1774: Estate Sizes and
Composition for Free Wealth-Holders (in sterling)

	All Colonies	New England	Middle Colonies	South
Mean average	£252.0	£161.2	£189.2	£394.7
Median average	108.7	74.4	152.5	144.5
Distribution:				
Bottom 20%	0.8%	1.0%	1.2%	0.7%
Top 20%	67.3%	65.9%	52.7%	69.6%
Composition:				
Land	53.0%	71.4%	60.5%	45.9%
Slave and servants	22.1%	0.5%	4.1%	33.6%
Livestock	9.2%	7.5%	11.3%	8.8%
Consumer-personal	6.7%	11.2%	8.4%	5.1%

SOURCE: Alice Hanson Jones, *American Colonial Wealth: Documents and Methods*,
2d ed., 3 vols. (New York: Arno Press, 1978). Tables in vol. 3.

wealth except perhaps clothing and a few personal items; meanwhile they were human assets owned by one segment of the white population. In the early 1770s, adult male slaves were valued at from £55 ($3,575) to £70 ($4,550) in Virginia. Slaves did have incomes, however, as measured by food consumption, clothing and housing allocations, wood burned for cooking and heating, medical services received, and minor incidentals. My estimate of slave incomes at £7 ($455) represents 54 percent of the income of the typical white nonslaveholder and 48 percent of the income of the typical slaveholder. The per capita incomes of nonslaveholding southerners were typically about £13 ($845), compared to £14.5 ($945) for members of slaveholding households with two adult bondsmen. The typical slaveholder by expropriating roughly one-half of the output of two slaves could raise family income by 10 to 15 percent. Even without the advantage of slave ownership, however, white incomes in the south were higher than in New England and on a par with the middle colonies.

The southern colonies possessed the largest share of colonial wealth, followed by the middle colonies and New England. Table 8.2 reveals that the south held 55.3 percent of the total physical wealth in probated estates in 1774. Even when slave wealth is excluded from the calculations, the ranking of the three regions remains the same. The south held 45.6 percent of nonhuman physical wealth, although the existence of slavery in the region may have contributed to increasing the value of other assets, especially land. The New England colonies had the lowest wealth totals whether measured in nonhuman (25.1 percent) or total physical wealth (20.3 percent).

The distribution of regional income favored the southern colonies by an even wider margin. The south generated 58.4 percent of aggregate colonial income. The inclusion of slave incomes in the calculations is the factor which propels the region's share of income three percentage points higher than its share of total physical wealth. Table 8.3 reveals that the middle colonies accounted for 23 percent of aggregate colonial

TABLE 8.2.   Regional Distribution of Physical Wealth, 1774 (in sterling)

	Free Population	Nonhuman Wealth[a]	%	Total Wealth	%
Southern Colonies	652,585	£40,225	45.6	£ 60,533	55.3
Middle Colonies	585,149	25,798	29.3	26,793	24.4
New England	582,285	22,116	25.1	22,232	20.3
Total	1,820,019	£88,139	100.0	£109,558	100.0

Per capita wealth plus *mean* income estimates based on a capital-to-output ratio of 3.5 : 1 assumed by Alice Hanson Jones, all colonies.

	Wealth	Mean Income
Nonhuman assets only[a]	£48.4	£13.8
Total physical wealth	60.2	17.2

SOURCE: Data derived from table 3.7 in Alice Hanson Jones, *Wealth of a Nation To Be: The American Colonies on the Eve of the Revolution* (New York: Columbia University Press, 1980).
[a] Nonhuman wealth does not include value of slaves and indentured servants in probated estates.

income, while New England trailed with a share of only 18.5 percent. The mean average for the free population, which was 99.2 percent white, was just over £17 ($1,105); the inclusion of slaves and indentured servants in the calculations reduces the mean average to just under £15 ($975).* These figures were extraordinarily high for a preindustrial society.

Based on the value of estates, the largest number of very wealthy men lived in the south. The average value of the estates of the top 1 percent of southern wealth-holders was £2,646 ($172,000), a figure over twice the size of the largest estates in the northern colonies. The first American millionaires had apparently emerged by the eighteenth century. The largest probated estate in the Jones sample belonged to Peter Manigault, a South Carolina planter and lawyer, who listed total assets of £27,958 ($1.8 million). Even with slaves excluded, Manigault still possessed the largest estate, for his nonhuman assets were recorded at £16,108 ($1.0 million). Indeed, nine of the largest fifteen colonial estates based solely on *nonhuman* assets were from the south in the Jones sample; and eight of the nine were from South Carolina.

The percentage of wealth-holders in the free population was fairly uniform in all three major regions, ranging from 23.5 to 24.5 percent. Women comprised from 8 to 10 percent of all wealth-holders, but the mean value of their estates was about one-half of the male figure, largely because they rarely owned land. The richest woman in the Jones sample was Abigail Townsend, who lived outside of Charleston and listed assets of £2,559 ($166,000).

Land was the most important asset in colonial estates. In New England, it accounted for 71 percent of wealth and in the middle colonies for 60 percent (table 8.1). In the southern colonies, Alice Hanson Jones's minimal figure for land is 46 percent, with slaves at around 34

---

* Readers should not be confused just because these mean averages are higher than the median estimates used earlier in the chapter to describe the living standards of the *typical* white family; the figures are not inconsistent, merely two different types of averages.

TABLE 8.3.   Regional Distribution of Income, 1774 (in sterling)

	Population	Per capita Income (Mean)[a]	Aggregate Income	%
Southern Colonies				
Free population	652,585	£26.5	£17,293,000	49.3
Slaves	433,106	7.0	3,032,000	8.6
Indentures	19,786	9.0	178,000	0.5
Subtotal	1,105,477		20,503,000	58.4
Middle Colonies				
Free population	585,149	13.1	7,665,000	21.8
Slaves	34,172	7.0	239,000	0.7
Indentures	21,374	9.0	192,000	0.5
Subtotal	640,695		8,096,000	23.0
New England				
Free population	582,285	10.8	6,289,000	17.9
Slaves	13,654	7.0	96,000	0.3
Indentures	11,856	9.0	107,000	0.3
Subtotal	607,795		6,492,000	18.5
Total	2,353,967		£35,091,000	

SOURCE: Data on free population compiled from information in table 3.7 in Jones, *Wealth of a Nation To Be.*
NOTE: Mean income estimates for the free population based on a capital-to-income ratio of 3.5:1 assumed by Alice Hanson Jones. However, estimates for per capita estimates of slave and indenture incomes are my own and are *not* based on the Jones data.
[a] Mean income, free and nonfree = £14.91 ($969)
   Mean income, free only   = £17.17 ($1,116)

percent. The composition of estates varied according to size. In the north, land and personal items were the two most important assets in small estates [under £100 ($6,500)], but land as a percentage of wealth rose steadily as the size of the estate increased. In the south, livestock (30 percent) and personal items (21 percent) were the most valuable assets in small estates. Land (42 percent) outranked slaves (28 percent) in medium estates (£100—399); and in the largest southern estates [over £400 ($26,000)], land (48 percent) and slaves (35 percent) comprised over four-fifths of the total assets.

The wealthest occupational group in the thirteen colonies was "esquires, gentleman, and officials," with mean asset holdings of £572 ($37,000). Table 8.4 shows that merchants were the second most prosperous group, followed by farmers with ancillary income (i.e., great southern planters); professionals such as doctors, lawyers, and ministers; farmers with no outside income plus fisherman; shopkeepers and innkeepers; and artisans and chandlers. The middle colonies displayed no significant deviations from the general pattern, but New England and the south revealed some differences. Merchants ranked first in New England, while the inclusion of fishermen in category 3 may help explain why that group fared so poorly in the New England standings. In the south, in contrast, farmers with ancillary income—or great planters—were the second wealthiest group after "esquires, gentlemen, and officials." Southern merchants dropped to fifth place in that region's occupational rankings, reflecting the small role of urban areas in the southern economy. For the thirteen colonies overall, it is notable that the mean wealth for all wealth-holders at

TABLE 8.4. Mean Value of Physical Wealth Held by Socioeconomic
Groups, 1774 (in sterling)

Wealth-Holder	Thirteen Colonies	New England	Middle Colonies	South
All Wealth-Holders	252.0	161.2	186.8	394.7
1. Esquires, gentlemen, and officials	572.4	313.4	1,233.0	1,281.3
2. Merchants	497.1	563.1	858.0	314.0
3. Farmers with ancillary income, plus fishermen	410.5	144.2	257.3	801.7
4. Professionals	341.0	270.6	240.6	512.2
5. Farmers and small planters with no outside income	262.3	155.3	179.8	396.1
6. Shopkeepers, innkeepers	204.3	219.0	221.7	194.7
7. Artisans, chandlers	122.5	114.5	144.5	137.8

SOURCE: Compiled from data in table 7.5 in Jones, Wealth of a Nation To Be.

£252 ($16,000), and for farmers and small planters at £262 ($17,000), were almost identical figures. The data reinforces once again our image of the average northerner as a family farmer and, in the south, as a small, nonslaveholding planter.

The data on the relationship between urban and rural wealth-holding are subject to different interpretations. From one standpoint, urban wealth appears to be higher; but from another vantage point, rural wealth comes out on top. Measured strictly on a *regional* basis, urban dwellers uniformly held more wealth than rural residents. In New England, urban wealth-holders held assets of £191 ($12,400), compared to only £151 ($9,800) for rural wealth-holders; in the middle colonies, the comparable figures were £287 ($18,600) for urban and £173 ($11,250) for rural wealth-holders; and for the south, they were £641 ($41,650) for urban and £392 ($25,500) for rural wealth-holders. On the basis of this analysis of wealth-holding in each section, urban dwellers appear to have held more assets.

Yet, when we aggregate the wealth data for the entire thirteen colonies, surprisingly overall rural wealth at £255 ($16,600) slightly edges urban wealth at £232 ($15,100). How could the outcome for the whole thirteen colonies appear to contradict the results in all three individual regions? A logical explanation exists. The reversal in order comes about because the rural wealth-holding figure for free southerners is so high at £392 and actually exceeds the wealth-holding of urban residents in the northern colonies. Because the south had the largest rural population, the southern figure had the greatest influence over the final average for the thirteen colonies. Simultaneously, the high urban figure for the south (£641) exerted a very small influence upon the overall urban average, since the northern colonies held the vast majority of the continent's urban residents. Again, the wealth figures for northern urban dwellers was significantly lower than the comparable figures for rural southerners. As a result, when all the data are aggregated, rural residents held 90 percent of the wealth in the colonies and urban dwellers only 10 percent; on a per family basis, rural wealth-holders averaged about 9 percent more assets than their urban counterparts. Generally speaking, we must be careful in defining whether we are discussing rural versus urban wealth-holding on a regional or continental basis before rendering judgments.

Wealth was concentrated in the hands of the elite classes throughout the thirteen colonies. One measure of the degree of concentration is the percentage of wealth held by the top 20 percent of wealth-holders. For the colonies overall, this group held 68 percent of the total assets. The regional breakdown was as follows: middle colonies—53 percent; New England—66 percent; and the southern colonies—70 percent (Table 8.1). The pattern of concentration usually emerged fairly rapidly after initial settlement. In one study of New England, Bruce Daniels found that wealth was largely in the hands of an elite class in most towns within forty years of their establishment. In Boston, for example, the concentration of wealth was about the same in the 1770s as it had been in 1700, with the upper 30 percent of wealth-holders owning from 85 to 90 percent of all taxable property.

Despite the existence of widespread slavery in the southern colonies, the pattern of wealth distribution was not significantly different in the south than in New England, where slaves were few in number. Southern wealth-holders in the top 20 percent claimed only 4 percent more of their region's assets than their counterparts in New England. Slavery was then only one of many factors accounting for the skewed distribution of wealth in the south; and indeed, even in its absence, the pattern of concentration might not have changed significantly. In the middle colonies, which had the widest distribution of wealth, the top 20 percent of wealth-holders still claimed over one-half of all assets. Meanwhile, although one-fifth of all wealth-holders owned over 65 percent of the total physical assets, this pattern of concentration was no impediment to the realization of the highest incomes levels in the world for the typical white family.

Over the last two decades, scholars have debated whether a trend toward greater inequality in wealth distribution emerged during the eighteenth century. The initial research, based on an analysis of tax lists in major port cities, indicated that the upper classes had suc-

158   MONEY AND TAXES

ceeded in accumulating a larger share of community assets as the
decades passed. But later, Gerard Warden discovered flaws in the application of the tax-list methodology in Boston, primarily because of
inconsistencies in the valuation of taxable assets over time. After recal-
culating the Boston figures to reflect the differences in valuation
procedures, Warden showed that wealth concentration had changed
very little in the eighteenth century; in 1681, the top 10 percent of
wealth-holders owned 42.3 percent of the taxable assets, while in 1771
their share had increased to only 47.5 percent. The difference was too
small to establish a clear-cut trend.

More recent studies concentrate mainly on data from probated
estates. In their broad survey of long-term trends in the distribution of
wealth in the United States, Jeffrey Williamson and Peter Lindert discovered that the distribution of wealth remained surprisingly stable
over the entire colonial era. They focused mainly on the interior towns
and counties, rather than on the major port cities and the densely settled regions along the coast. These interior areas contained over 90
percent of the total population. Williamson and Lindert found that the
constant opening up of new frontier regions, where wealth distribution
was invariably more equitable, generally offset any movement toward
greater concentration in the most heavily urban areas. While conced-
ing that the wealth shares of the elite merchant class might have risen
in a few isolated areas like Philadelphia and Worchester County,
Massachusetts, and might have triggered local demands for revolution
and social change, they emphasized that these areas were atypical.
Indeed, urban residents declined as a percentage of the colonial population after 1700. In sharp contrast to the increasing rate of wealth
inequality characteristic of the nineteenth century, Williamson and
Lindert concluded that the overall distribution of wealth showed no
measureable trend in the colonial period.

Living space in the typical colonial home with five members was
cramped. In Philadelphia in the 1770s, Sam Bass Warner found the
average artisan or shopkeeper lived in a narrow, story-and-a-half
structure with about 800 square feet of space. The owner usually used

the largest front room as a work area. In Germantown, Pennsylvania, Stephanie Wolf discovered about the same total living space available in most houses, although small-town artisans normally worked away from the home in separate buildings.

Homes did not have indoor plumbing, and a fireplace provided all the cooking and heating facilities. A few beds, chairs, stools, and cabinets were the usual furnishing. In slave quarters, which accounted for about 20 percent of family living units by the 1770s, houses were furnished with straw bedding and barrels for chairs. Candles and whale oil lamps provided the lighting. The only methods of preserving food were salting, smoking, and drying. In urban areas, water came from shallow wells, which were occasionally contaminated, since no town had water pipes or sewage lines.

The personal property of the typical white colonist was limited as well. A few items of handmade clothing, including one or two wool garments for winter, and a pair of shoes were the basic wardrobe. The lower classes frequently ate from wooden bowls. By the eighteenth century, most middle-class families owned earthenware, some bed and table linen, knives, forks, and a Bible. A family with income above the median might possess a few fancy clothes, a watch, china plates, fine furniture, some silver items, and other small amenities. The wealthy often owned fine clothes and furniture, exquisite china and silverware, nonreligious books, a man's wig, artwork, a carriage, and a large volume of luxury goods. The wealthy usually had servants or slaves to perform routine household tasks.

RISING INCOMES

Although the picture of colonial living standards on the eve of independence has now come into sharper focus, it remains less clear how much those standards changed over the seventeenth and eighteenth centuries and when improvements in average incomes might have occurred. About two decades ago, scholars began thinking more seriously about American economic growth prior to industrialization, and the consensus then was that individual incomes had probably grown negligibly, if at all, before 1840. This view of stagnation in incomes has undergone substantial modification in recent years. Phyllis Deane and W. A. Cole found, for example, that average incomes in England had risen slowly but steadily at rates from 3 to 8 percent a decade between 1700 and 1780, long before industrialization had made much impact on the British economy. Meanwhile, American scholars—among them George Rogers Taylor, Robert Gallman, and Paul David—pushed back the onset of per capita growth in the United States to at least the 1820s and 1830s, and it was hypothesized that some growth might have occurred during the colonial era after all.

The data is still fragmentary but the best guess now is that colonial incomes clearly rose, and at a rate of .3 to .5 percent a year over the entire 150 year period. This figure is only a fraction of the growth rates of 3 to 5 percent experienced by many advanced economies today, but in the context of the seventeenth and eighteenth centuries, the performance was laudatory, since only in England, Holland, and North America were population and per capita incomes actually rising simultaneously.

The beginning of income growth in the colonies was in the seventeenth century, according to recent studies by Terry Anderson and Russell Menard. From 1650 to 1709, Anderson argued that average incomes in New England rose at an annual rate of perhaps 1.6 percent, with a lower figure of 1 percent the absolute minimum, allowing for as much as a 50 percent margin of error. The average value of estates rose one-third over the last half of the century, with the largest percentage increase occurring in the 1670s. Anderson's data suggest that living standards in New England in 1700 were already 75 percent of those in 1774, which translates into a per capita income of about £9 ($585) in 1700.

In the eighteenth century, in contrast, Anderson cited evidence indicating that the rate of income growth per capita had slowed appreciably. In a detailed analysis of Hampshire County, Massachusetts, from 1700 to 1779, he discovered that a population boom offset much of the rise in aggregate output and held the increase in living standards to no more than 3 percent a decade. The size of the typical household in Hampshire climbed from 4.6 members in 1691/1715 to 6.4 members in 1761/80. The relatively weaker performance of the economy in this region reinforced Anderson's view that New England experienced greater gains in productivity during the previous century.

Meanwhile, Russell Menard's research on the Chesapeake region revealed that individual incomes rose rapidly in the 1630s, progressed gradually in the period from 1640 to 1670, and then remained steady over the remainder of the century. Productivity increased continuously in tobacco farming, with the number of plants one man could cultivate jumping threefold from 1630 to 1700. The introduction of standardized shipping containers aided in reducing freight costs by one-half in the late 1620s and early 1630s, while the expense of marketing tobacco in England fell from 10 percent to 2.5 percent by the end of the century. Per capita incomes failed to move upward at the same rate after 1640, however, because of a sharp rise in the dependency ratio—which is the ratio of total population to taxables (adult males). Males increasingly shared their newfound prosperity with wives, children, and relatives; the dependency ratio increased from 1.34 to 3.42 between 1625 and 1712. The rises in productivity and dependency generally offset one another and kept per capita incomes in the tobacco regions at about the same level from 1670 to 1720.

The accumulation of evidence pointing to a continued rise in living standards over the eighteenth century is also varied but fairly persuasive when considered jointly. At the more abstract quantitative level, a comparison of the mean values of New England estates calculated by Alice Jones for 1774 with the same figures generated by Terry Anderson for 1700 are consistent with the hypothesis that wealth rose at a rate of just over 5 percent a decade. Since Bruce Daniels has argued that the concentration of wealth did not change significantly over the eighteenth century, the conclusion that the incomes of the typical New Englander increased at about the same rate as wealth accumulated appears reasonable.

Some of the most persuasive evidence comes out of the research of Duane Ball and Gary Walton on agricultural productivity in the middle colonies. An assessment of productivity changes in the agricultural sector is critical, because farming accounted for the lion's share of colonial output. Based on a detailed study of Chester County, Pennsylvania, which was southwest of Philadelphia, Ball and Walton estimated that agricultural productivity per se rose about 2 percent a decade in the eighteenth century and that collateral nonagricultural activities added perhaps another 1 percent to the total. Indeed, few scholars now support growth figures any lower than the Ball and Walton calculation of a 3 percent rise per decade in living standards.

In a recent survey of economic growth in the Chesapeake region from 1704 to 1776, Allan Kulikoff found the per capita growth in overall wealth was 4 percent a decade in Prince George's County, Maryland. The timing of growth in the tobacco regions was almost the reverse of the pattern in the northern colonies. Whereas most scholars have cited the first half of the eighteenth century as the main period for income growth in the north, Kulikoff concluded that growth was slow until mid-century in the Chesapeake colonies but then accelerated rapidly from 1755 to 1775.

In a study of the changing asset composition of estates in St. Mary's County, Maryland, between the seventeenth and eighteenth centuries, Lois Green Carr and Lorena Walsh discovered clear signs of improving living standards. In the seventeenth century, the typical family owned little furniture and few personal items. Over the next century, however, the number of amenities in estate inventories went up. Carr and Walsh made a list of twelve common amenities and traced their frequency in two periods—1658–1702 and 1703–77. Whereas the typical estate before 1702 listed only two to three of these amenities, after that date the number was four to six. In the seventeenth century, the only two items listed in one-half of all estates were earthenware and linen, but after 1703 the list had expanded to include knives, forks, and religious books as well. In the largest estates, spices, secular books, clocks and watches, and maps turned up much more often in the eighteenth century. The median value of estates in St. Mary's County rose sharply from £42 ($2,700) in 1703–15 to £87 ($5,700) in 1755–77.

Other scholars have sought to identify areas of increasing productivity plus other factors which might have accounted for eighteenth-century income growth. James Shepherd and Gary Walton concentrated on improvements in transportation and distribution. The suppression of piracy in colonial waters eliminated the need for space-consuming armaments and larger crews. Insurance costs likewise fell. They also found that raw materials were handled and processed more efficiently; for example, the tighter compression of tobacco in packing boosted the weight of a hogshead by one-third. The increased volume of trade reduced the number of idle days that ships spent in port collecting cargoes. The cost of borrowing to buy imported goods from England declined as well; interest rates in London fell during the eighteenth century and American consumers were among the beneficiaries.

Marc Egnal has also argued that, in addition to increased agricultural productivity, the colonies gained from a favorable shift in the terms of trade. First, the introduction of the "cradle" scythe around 1750 permitted some farmers to harvest more grain than formerly. More important, however, the market prices of agricultural products, which were the colonies' main exports, climbed steadily after 1760 while the prices of English manufactured goods remained roughly the same. In the 1740s, 100 bushels of colonial wheat could be exchanged for 150 yards of woolen cloth, but by the early 1760s, Egnal observed, an identical 100 bushels bought 250 yards of the same material, a two-thirds increase. The per capita purchases of imports rose from £.65 ($42) in 1743–47 to £1.49 ($97) in 1758–62. As the prices of the foodstuffs that the colonists sold abroad rose in relation to the prices of the foreign goods they consumed, living standards went up. Yet, because foreign trade involved only 10 to 13 percent of colonial output, the contribution to overall living standards were fairly limited. John Hanson estimates a gain of perhaps one-half of 1 percent annually in the period from 1745 to 1760.

Finally, we have the estimates of Alice Hanson Jones. Based on the assumption that the growth in incomes corresponded closely with increases in the size of probated estates, she calculated annual growth rates for three distinct periods: 1650 to 1725—.3 percent; 1725 to 1750—.4 percent; and 1750 to 1775—.5 percent. Jones concluded in *Wealth of a Nation To Be* that "despite possible local or regional spurts or lags or even actual declines in some subperiods, there was from 1650 on an overall fairly steady rate of intensive growth for all regions combined." Significantly, her data indicate that living standards advanced more slowly in the seventeenth century. Only New England appears to have experienced a possible slowing in productivity during the eighteenth century; in this respect, her findings are generally compatible with those of Terry Anderson and Bruce Daniels. Most important, however, Jones estimated that per capita incomes were not only rising but that the rate of growth was accelerating during the half-century before independence.

In sum, the overall performance of the colonial economy in terms of extensive growth and the standard of living achieved for the white population was unmatched in the eighteenth century. England and Holland were also experiencing per capita growth, but neither was absorbing the same rate of population growth as the thirteen colonies. The highest average incomes in the world for the free population combined with growth rates on a par with its only two rivals, and all in the face of a population boom at close to the reproductive maximum for the species—these were the unique colonial characteristics.

By the early 1770s, the colonial gross product was around £35 million ($2.3 billion) annually. It was roughly 40 percent of the figure for the mother country. Moreover, the colonies were rapidly gaining on England, for just three-quarters of a century earlier, in 1700, their gross product had been a trifling 4 percent of England's. Parliament was surely right when it determined that the thirteen North American colonies were strong enough to pay additional taxes for their own defense. On the other hand, the colonies also had ample economic resources to steer an independent course.

BIBLIOGRAPHICAL   ESSAY

The best sources of data on colonial wealth are the scholarly works of Alice Hanson Jones; see her *American Colonial Wealth: Documents and Methods*, 3 vols., 2d ed. (New York: Arno Press, 1978)—the second edition has the revised southern figures in a special appendix—and her analysis of the data in *Wealth of a Nation To Be: The American Colonies on the Eve of the Revolution* (New York: Columbia University Press, 1980). Other studies of the distribution of wealth are Bruce Daniels, "Long Range Trends of Wealth Distribution in Eighteenth-Century New England," *Explorations in Economic History* (Winter 1973/74), pp. 123–35, and Jeffrey Williamson and Peter Lindert, "Long Term Trends in American Wealth Inequality," Discussion Paper #472-77, Institute for Research on Poverty (Madison: University of Wisconsin, 1977).

Two books describing the middle-class status of colonial Americans are Jackson Turner Main, *The Social Structure of Revolutionary America* (Princeton, N.J.: Princeton University Press, 1965) and Richard Hofstadter's posthumous, uncompleted volume, *America at 1750: A Social Portrait* (New York: Vintage, 1973). For information on living standards in the north, I relied heavily on Sam Bass Warner, *The Private City: Philadelphia in Three Periods of Its Growth* (Philadelphia: University of Pennsylvania Press, 1968); Stephanie Wolf, *Urban Village: Population, Community, and Family Structure in Germantown, Pennsylvania, 1683–1800* (Princeton N.J.: Princeton University Press, 1976); and Billy Smith, "The Best Poor Man's Country: Living Standards of the Lower Sort in Late Eighteenth-

Century Philadelphia," in Glenn Porter and William Mulligan, eds., in the series Working Papers from the Regional Economic History Research Center, vol. 2, no. 4 (Greenville, Del., 1979). I also used James Lemon, "Household Consumption in Eighteenth-Century America and Its Relationship to Production and Trade: The Situation among Farmers in Southeastern Pennsylvania," *Agricultural History*, (January 1967), 41:59–70, and Karen Friedmann, "Victualling Colonial Boston," *ibid.* (July 1973), pp. 189–205. For the south, see Aubrey C. Land, "Economic Base and Social Structure: The Northern Chesapeake in the Eighteenth Century," *Journal of Economic History* (December 1965), pp. 639–54, and Paul Clemens, "The Operation of an Eighteenth-Century Chesapeake Tobacco Plantation," *Agricultural History* (July 1975), pp. 517–31. The data on height and nutrition is from Kenneth Sokoloff and Georgia Villaflor, "Colonial and Revolutionary Muster Rolls:'Some New Evidence on Nutrition and Migration in Early America," Working Paper #374, National Bureau of Economic Research (Cambridge, Mass., 1979).

For an introduction to the controversy about the rate of growth in per capita incomes in the colonies, see George Rogers Taylor, "American Economic Growth before 1840: An Exploratory Essay," *Journal of Economic History* (December 1964), pp. 427–44; Paul David, "The Growth of Real Product in the United States before 1840: New Evidence and Controlled Conjectures," *ibid.* (June 1967), pp. 151–97; Robert Gallman, "The Pace and Pattern of American Economic Growth," in Lance Davis et al., *American Economic Growth: An Economist's History of the United States* (New York: Harper & Row, 1972); and Elliot Brownlee, *Dynamics of Ascent: A History of the American Economy* (New York: Knopf, 1974), pp. 1–82. For data on England, see Phyllis Deane and W. A. Cole, *British Economic Growth, 1688–1959*, 2nd ed. (Cambridge: Cambridge University Press, 1967).

The most comprehensive article on the mainland colonies is Marc Egnal, "The Economic Development of the Thirteen Continental Colonies, 1720 to 1775," *William and Mary Quarterly* (April 1975) pp. 191–222. A rebuttal of his thesis is John R. Hanson, "The Economic Development of the Thirteen Colonies, 1720 to 1775: A Critique," *ibid.*, in press. For New England in the seventeenth century, see Terry Anderson and Robert Paul Thomas, "White Population, Labor Force, and Extensive Growth of the New England Economy in the Seventeenth Century," *Journal of Economic History* (September 1973), pp. 634–61; Anderson, "Economic Growth in Colonial New England: 'Statistical Renaissance,'" *ibid.* (March 1979), pp. 243–57; and Anderson, *The Economic Growth of Seventeenth-Century New England: A Measurement of Regional Income* (New York: Arno Press, 1975). An important article on the middle colonies is Duane Ball and Gary Walton, "Agricultural Productivity Change in Eighteenth-Century Pennsylvania," *Journal of Economic History* (March 1976), pp. 102–17.

Three excellent papers on the tobacco region were given at a conference at the Eleutherian Mills Library in Greenville, Delaware, in 1977. They were later published in Glenn Porter and William Mulligan, eds., *Economic Change in the Chesapeake Colonies,* Working Papers from the Regional Economic History Research Center, vol. I, no. 3 (Greenville, Del., 1978): Russell Menard, "Secular Trends in the Chesapeake Tobacco Industry," pp. 1–34; P. M. G. Harris, "Integrating Interpretations of Local and Regionwide Change in the Study of Economic Development and Demographic Growth in the Colonial Chesapeake, 1630–1775," pp. 35–71; and Lois Green Carr and Lorena S. Walsh, "Changing Life Styles in Colonial St. Mary's County," pp. 73–118. Allan Kulikoff stresses economic growth in the third quarter of the eighteenth century in "The Economic Growth of the Eighteenth-Century Chesapeake Colonies," *Journal of Economic History* (March 1979), pp. 275–288.

The sources of productivity growth in the trade sector are identified in James Shepherd and Gary Walton, *Shipping, Maritime Trade, and the Economic Development of Colonial North America* (Cambridge: Cambridge University Press, 1972). A thorough discussion of the literature on per capita growth rates is found in chapter 7 of Alice Hanson Jones's *Wealth of a Nation To Be,* which was cited in the first paragraph of this essay.

APPENDIX

NOTE ON PRICE AND INCOME
ESTIMATES

The conversion of sterling prices into current U.S. dollars is based on the data series in Alice Hanson Jones, *American Colonial Wealth,* 3:1719, table 3.5, which carries the exchange ratio up to 1975. By that date, one pound in British sterling was valued at $45.19. I have adjusted that figure upward for changes in the consumer price index for 1975–78 and finally projected for anticipated inflation rates of 10 percent annually in 1979 and 1980. My conversion ratio is $65 to one pound sterling. Such figures are not precise but do serve as useful guidelines for relating monetary values in the colonial era to prices and income in modern times.

The same degree of tenativeness applies to estimates of incomes and living standards in the colonial period. The estimates of mean incomes in this book are based on the application of a 3.5 to 1 capital-to-output ratio. The capital figures are the wealth data from the research of Alice Hanson Jones. For a discussion of why she selected the ratio of 3.5 to 1 as the most appropriate for colonial America, see Appendix A in her new book, *Wealth of a Nation To Be* (Columbia University Press, 1980).

The estimates of median incomes for typical farmers and slaves in the south are my own. My decision to abandon mean averages in describing the incomes of these groups was based on the very skewed distribution of assets among southern wealth-holders. The application of a 3.5 to 1 capital-to-output ratio to free southern wealth-holders produces a mean income of £26.5 ($1,725). That figure seems too high in describing the living standards of the typical southern white. It is difficult to believe that southern whites had incomes twice those in the northern colonies, especially when the Jones data also reveals that median wealth in the south was actually 5.3 percent *below* the median figure for the middle colonies.

For the New England and middle colonies, where the aggregate value of the assets held by the top 20 percent of wealth-holders was a much lower amount than in the south, I have assumed that differences between mean and median incomes were quite modest. In discussing the incomes and living standards of northern residents, I have used the mean and median averages interchangeably. In describing the south, my review of the evidence about the productivity of the typical family farm, with no bonded labor, suggested that output was not very much different from that in the middle colonies. The closeness of the median wealth figures for the two regions also encouraged me in this view.

Estimating the incomes of slaves and slaveholders required more imagination. For slaves, I began with an analysis of diet. Several sources indicate that the cost of providing an adequate diet, including about one-half pound of meat per week, ranged from £3 to £4. Food generally accounted for 50 percent of the cost of maintaining a slave; slaves also received income in kind from the receipt of coarse clothing, a housing allotment, and medical services. Many slaves had sufficient free time to chop wood for cooking and heating. (In his study of lower-class workers in Philadelphia, Billy Smith discovered that urban families typically spent 10 percent of income on wood energy.) I finally settled on a figure of £7 per capita for slaves, which translates into about $455 in 1980 or $2,275 for a family unit of five.

In estimating the incomes of typical slaveholders, I assumed that slaves produced on average the same output as free white farmers and that an owner and bondsman divided about equally the fruits of slave labor. The rate of exploitation was much higher than the rate of profit on slave ownership, however, because part of the output extracted forcibly from slaves went to cover the cost of the original capital investment. By acquiring two slaves, the typical slaveholding family could probably raise its living standards by 10 to 15 percent. By thereby expropriating slave income, members of a typical slaveholding family had incomes of around £14.5 ($945).

INDEX

174